WHAT EVERY CHRISTIAN SHOULD KNOW

The Christianity Today Series:

The Sexual Christian, by Tim Stafford

Tough Questions Christians Ask, David Neff, editor

The Blackboard Fumble, Ken Sidey, editor

What Every Christian Should Know,
by Jo H. Lewis and Gordon A. Palmer

WHAT EVERY CHRISTIAN SHOULD KNOW

JO H. LEWIS &
GORDON A. PALMER

VICTOR BOOKS®
A DIVISION OF SCRIPTURE PRESS PUBLICATIONS INC.
USA CANADA ENGLAND

Recommended Dewey Decimal Classification: 268
Suggested Subject Heading: CHRISTIAN EDUCATION

Library of Congress Catalog Card Number: 89-60143
ISBN: 0-89693-711-9

Cover Illustration: Tim Jonke

CONTENTS

ACKNOWLEDGMENTS

We want particularly to thank Jo Lewis's husband, Johndy, whose commitment to, and computer support for, this project never flagged. Along with him, her daughter, Rebecca Psyhos, gave sound criticism of several versions of the entire manuscript; she provided the bulk of the reading list.

We want also to thank the research department of *Christianity Today* and the Christianity Today Institute Fellows and Scholars. The editors—Rodney Clapp, Timothy Jones, and David Neff—pushed us throughout to reevaluate what we were writing and to cut through to the gist of what we wanted to say. Errors in accuracy, nevertheless, are our own.

Others who gave substantive direction were Mark Wade, Judy Grover, Paul Romoser, Bruce Hicks, Dean Hennings, David Robinson, and Gordon Palmer's wife and son, Vivian and David, as well as Sara White and other family members. Essential help also came from the Haviland (Kansas) Friends Church; the Chancel Choir, First Presbyterian Church, Arlington Heights, Illinois; and the students of Trinity College and Friends Bible College, especially Heidi Longstroth and Pam Neifert (who helped with research and manuscript preparation).

The encouragement and prayers of these and other colleagues and friends—knowledgeable Christians all—sustained us through the project.

FOREWORD

Americans have the worldwide reputation for wanting to be biggest and best—in everything. Sometimes this braggadocio creates resentment. More often it is accepted with amused tolerance—especially, for example, when we boast of our great orchestras playing Bach, Beethoven, and Brahms.

Historically, Americans have been most proud of their achievement in education. "Universal education for democracy" is our motto, and I was an ardent chanter of the slogan.

For me, disillusionment set in during a year of postgraduate study in Germany where, for the first time, I learned the facts of life regarding educational excellence. By the time German youngsters reach the fourth grade, I learned, they are a full academic year ahead of their American counterparts. From there, the disparity accelerates. The average German *high school* graduate knows twice as much as the average American *college* graduate.

Something is radically wrong

The first warning signal that something was radically wrong with the American educational system was the Soviet space satellite, *Sputnik*. How could Russian science and technology produce high-quality space technology so quickly? Obviously their success could only rest on a broad base of advanced studies in math and science. The cry went up for more math and science in American high schools. But after the first spasm of wounded pride had subsided, few further constructive changes were made. The American system rolled on undisturbed and uncorrected.

Then, in the eighties, a series of studies exploded our complacency. American children, we discovered, were simply not learning. Every study showed, with sickening regularity, that American high school graduates fall at the bottom of the scale of major nations (with Sweden and Japan at the top). Our graduates do not understand basic mathematical concepts. They cannot read well enough to follow simple safety instructions. They cannot communicate ideas. They do not understand American history and culture—they know even less about world history and culture.

The effects of this tragic failure have been devastating. We pride ourselves on our free-market economy. But all of a sudden we were losing the battle for high-tech markets in TVs and computers. Even our hard-earned reputation for producing inexpensive, dependable automobiles was jeopardized. In spite of school systems filled with dedicated teachers, we have been unable to provide the minimal skills essential for a modern industrial, democratic power.

The case against American public education is easy to document. It begins in the earliest grades. In the 1920s, the average first-grade reader contained 645 different words. By the 1930s, this number had dropped to 460. Analyzing seven widely used grade-school readers published between 1960 and 1963, researchers discovered that "total pre-primary vocabulary ranged from a low of 54 to a high of 83 words; primary vocabularies, from 113 to 173 words."[1]

Most first-grade children use a vocabulary of over four thousand words. Even the lowest level of first graders knows well over two thousand words. Writing a century ago, Anne Sullivan, teacher of Helen Keller, noted bitterly: "Public education programs seem to be built on the supposition that every child is a kind of idiot." If that was true in her day, then in our day we must consider children five times more idiotic.

Required foreign-language courses have completely disappeared from public high schools. Most colleges and universities have discarded any foreign-language requirement either for admission or graduation. Scholastic Aptitude Test (SAT) scores have dropped almost every year. Between 1968 and 1980, they declined sixty-eight points. A slight increase in test scores for the last year or two is from such a low base that it is hardly encouraging.

Recently, a new, even more devastating factor has surfaced. Most students perform far below the level their ability scores predict. Today's best students score dramatically lower than their counterparts a decade ago. Out of a constant pool of approximately one million test takers, only one-quarter as many now score over 650 and only half as many above 600 on the SAT ratings. This comes from our brightest and best, our hope for tomorrow.

In 1981, the U.S. Department of Education created a blue-ribbon commission to see what could be done to halt this slippage. After a two-year study, the panel reported its findings in a book entitled *A Nation at Risk: The Imperative for Educational Reform*. The report is excellent, as far as it goes. It suggests many valuable palliatives for our present system:

1. A curriculum with "five new basics," including four years of high-school English, three years of math, science, and social studies, two years of foreign language, and one-half year of computer science, together with appropriate courses in the fine arts and vocational studies. That sort of requirement would put starch into the curriculum at every high school in all fifty states.
2. Higher standards, rigidly maintained.
3. More time in school. Increase the present six-hour day to eight, and the current 180-school-day year to 220 (the average for almost every industrial nation in the world).
4. Upgrading the preparation and performance of teachers.

Unfortunately, neither the dire predictions nor the good advice of the blue-ribbon panel halted the devastating decline in the quality of American education.

In 1987, E. D. Hirsch, Jr., a highly regarded authority in the field of hermeneutics and the meaning of language, published a volume that pinpointed what is, perhaps, the worst effect of this educational disaster (*Cultural Literacy: What Every American Should Know*). He called it cultural illiteracy. By that he means the lack of "basic information needed to thrive in the modern world." He accepts the devastating data of our failure to communicate our heritage to the younger generation and asks: "What are the consequences of this failure?" His answer: "Only by piling up specific, communally shared information can children learn to participate in complex cooperative activities with other members of their community."[2]

Long ago the Tower of Babel showed us that if we can't communicate with each other, we can't work together. Effective communication, as Hirsch demonstrates over and over again, requires not merely an ability to read and understand words, but a body of information as a meaningful context for discussion.

Hirsch blames John Dewey, a principal architect of American educational theory, who denigrated "the piling up of information." Useless facts, Dewey implied, are unnecessary to effective communication. Unfortunately, Dewey was taken seriously, and our children suffer accordingly. To communicate effectively, we need to know—and to know what others know. Shared information is the key. And this is just what our youngsters are not getting in school.

In the appendix to his volume, Hirsch lists approximately five thousand terms he believes would serve as a guide for rebuilding the information vacuum created by our Dewey-influenced schools. We must begin early in the educational process, Hirsch insists. By the fourth grade it is already too late. By then we have squandered younger children's unique ability to memorize data.

More warning signals were sounded. Also in 1987, Allan Bloom published *The Closing of the American Mind*. Once again, the American educational establishment was shaken. Bloom decried the movement in American culture that has led to the mass destruction of values. He called for a return to the true and the good—absolute truth and absolute good.

In the last century, American education has convinced our students that we cannot discover absolute truth, that democracy is optional, that there are no values worth fighting for. In earlier days, America's Founding Fathers taught the opposite.

Since ours was a land of freedom, we tolerated those who advocated these foreign ideas. But we knew they were wrong, and we tried to persuade them to think better.

In today's world, however, tolerance is not enough. True democracy, some say, demands that we not only tolerate ideas we believe to be wrong, but that we hold all ideas to be equally true and equally good: Respect even inane views. Don't condemn another's ideas as wrong or bad—especially, of course, the idea that ultimately all views are equally true for the people who hold them.

Bloom disagrees. Search for the true and the good, he says, and return to a liberal arts education that would reinform us of good ideas from the past. We must think and weigh ideas. He despairs "whether there is either the wherewithal or the energy within the university to constitute or reconstitute the ideal educated human being and establish a liberal education again."[3]

An evangelical crisis

What does all this have to do with evangelical Christianity? Everything! As James Hitchcock, professor of European history at St. Louis University, says, "What is at stake today is not merely the survival of a particular denominational group or of once privileged dogmas. What is at stake is the survival of all values and of any kind of belief. . . . What is at stake is the survival of humanity."

Evangelicals represent a significant part of our nation. If our *nation* cannot function effectively as a society, *we* cannot function effectively as a society. If our nation cannot participate in a democracy, we cannot participate in a democracy. If our nation is incapable of passing good and wise laws, we are incapable of passing good and wise laws. If our nation falls apart into disparate, isolated islands of individuals who cannot communicate effectively with one another, we too are isolated and cannot communicate with others.

As Americans, we have a wonderful heritage. We can despise it and let it die, or we can build on it. We can choose to live in a land of different values and different standards from those that our forebears bequeathed to us at such great sacrifice.

As evangelicals living in a democracy, we are both rulers and citizens in our land. Someday we shall have to face God and give account to him for our part, or lack of it, in the leadership of our nation. That includes what we have done about education in America. We cannot lightly ignore this responsibility.

Much of the culture we see disappearing before our eyes is precious to evangelicals. Our civilization has been deeply permeated with Christian faith. Bit by bit we now see those Christian influences being strained out of our culture. The National Institute of Education reports: "Religion, traditional family values, and conservative political and economic positions have been reliably excluded from children's text books . . . in grades one through four." These social-studies textbooks purport to introduce the child to society—to family life, community activities, economic transactions, and history. The report continues: "None of the books covering grades one through four contained a single word referring to any religious activity in contemporary life." From reading them you would conclude that the American people are an absolutely irreligious people.

Yet 94 percent of the American people say they believe in God, and 85 to 90 percent say they accept basic religious values. The report concludes:

> Not one word [of these textbooks] refers to any child or adult who prayed or went to any church or temple. The family was often mentioned in these books, but the idea that marriage is the origin and foundation of the family was never presented. Even the words marriage, wedding, husband, wife, did not occur once in these books. Nowhere was it suggested that being a mother or homemaker was a worthy or important role for a woman.

Evangelicals are concerned about the cultural illiteracy overwhelming our society, both because they have a special responsibility for the direction and well-being of our society and because we ourselves are an integral part of this culture, and when it suffers, we suffer.

What should we do?

We must ask ourselves: *What can we do to challenge our nation to turn back from so relentlessly pursuing this destructive path?* The Report of the President's Commission, E. D. Hirsch, Jr., and Allan Bloom point us in the right direction. Yet the task seems overwhelming. Still, there is one area in which every evangelical has a special responsibility. That is the Christian and spiritual heritage that played so large a part in our culture. These Christian influences embedded in our culture are critical to the communication of the gospel, to the retention of those values that are consistent with Christianity, and to the standards of life that allow for the gospel to be received with understanding and acceptance. It is harder and harder to communicate to the unbelieving world around us what we mean by sin and the gospel and our Christian standards of life. Our entire Christian world-and-life view becomes more and more unintelligible. People simply do not have an intellectual framework in which the Christian message makes sense. We need to reinvigorate or, if necessary, reintroduce these Christian vestiges of our common culture. If we do not fortify and deepen this religious heritage, evangelism will not prove much easier. It is the special task of evangelicals to seek to persuade our society how important those values are to them.

Unfortunately, the church itself has already lost this core. A Gallup poll reveals that 85 percent of the American people assent to the validity of the Ten Commandments. They not only believe the commandments are valid, but that some day all will have to answer to God for how they have obeyed or disobeyed them. Unbelievably, these same people don't know what the Ten Commandments are! Only a few can name as many as five. And, of course, even fewer obey them. Worst of all, evangelical Christians are little better than the general populace. They, too, have lost understanding of the basic moral law of God. Every church statistician or Christian educator I know laments that knowledge about religion, the Bible, and Christianity has fallen off even more severely than nonreligious information.

We are told that in the ancient world of the early church, theological topics were the stuff of common conversation. The barber in his Constantinople shop discussed with his customers whether Jesus Christ was of the same substance with the Father or only similar to the Father. Such a discussion is unthinkable today. It would even be unthinkable in a Sunday-school class for most of our churches. Some time ago I taught a Sunday-school class with my text drawn from the prologue to the Gospel of John. In the class, I did my best to unfold what the Bible teaches relating to the doctrine of the Trinity and how we as Christians today are to understand that doctrine. After the class, an earnest member (he happened to be a carpenter) came up to me to register his protest. "You know," he said, "I've been working hard all week. I didn't come to Sunday school this morning to hear a lecture in theology. I came to have my heart warmed."

Now, I am willing to take my share of blame for making a discussion of the Trinity into a dull class for that dissatisfied carpenter. But I cannot help registering my own counterprotest. Biblical Christianity is based on a personal revelation of God to humans and their response in faith, love, and obedience. Yet there is no genuine biblical faith without knowledge. We cannot have biblical Christianity without theology or right ideas.

Even in our evangelical Sunday schools we manage to avoid a clear understanding of our Christian faith. Lessons for young children are restricted to the kind heavenly Father who made the birds, bees, and butterflies (a very essential doctrine, mind you). But the biblical doctrine of sin is too abstract and ill suited to the minds of young children. And when they get older, all too often they are conditioned against the importance of doctrine. Only what is immediately and quickly digested and can be put into practice at the moment is considered valuable. Ethical issues have replaced doctrinal issues in most Sunday-school curriculums. The problem with that? We are seeking solutions to these ethical issues divorced from any basis in biblical theology.

Why is it important for us to know the basic facts of Christian faith? Because God in Scripture has commanded us to do so. Among the last words of the great lawgiver, Moses, were: "These words, which I am commanding you today, shall be on your heart; and you shall teach them diligently to your sons and shall talk of them when you sit in your house and when you walk by the way and when you lie down and when you rise up. And you shall bind them as a sign on your hand and they shall be as frontals on your forehead" (Deut. 6:6–9, NASB). The New Testament Scriptures reinforce this command: "And, fathers, do not provoke your children to anger; but bring them up in the discipline and instruction of the Lord" (Eph. 6:4, NASB). We need to know the facts of Bible history, the instruction in the Old and New Testaments, the basic structures of our Christian doctrine, the emotional tones conveyed by the Psalms, the penetrating insights of the Beatitudes, the stories in the Gospels, and the parables of our Lord. God commands it.

How? We need to memorize Scripture: the psalms of David in order to enter fully into the response of an obedient and loving heart to our sovereign and gracious God, and other verses of Scripture that will remain in the back of our minds as a framework for all our thought. We need to understand the salient facts of church history so that we may understand how the church has interpreted God's Word for each generation. We need encouragement drawn from the willingness of our predecessors to stand firmly for the truth in trying circumstances. And, of course, we need to understand key doctrines of our Christian faith so that they are intelligible in contemporary language and today's thought forms. The Lutheran catechism, the Westminster Confession and Catechism, Baptist catechisms, and the Anglican prayer book all served to shape the convictions and piety of Christians across the ages. Without these rich resources from the past, Christianity withers.

By introduction into Christian culture, moreover, we are tied into our own past. It gives us a home in the awesome, silent reaches of the universe. A child whose mind and heart have been filled with the rock-ribbed instruction of the Ten Commandments, the emotional releases that poured from the heart of David, the broad sweep of history conveying to us God's dealings with his people, and the moral insight found in the Beatitudes is prepared to face the world in a new and better way.

But how can we transmit this precious heritage of our biblical Christian faith when we do not even know what it is? Here, authors Jo Lewis and Gordon Palmer have come to our rescue. They have tried to meet this most desperate need in the Christian church today by surveying for us what are the most essential elements of our heritage that we must guard and hand on to our children and to future generations. Fortunately, they have not merely engaged in hand wringing over the plight of the church but have provided practical suggestions as to what our Christian people specifically must communicate to their children and what they need to know in order to understand a truly biblical faith. They have sought to present us with:

1. What we need in order to develop a mature appropriation of biblical and Christian faith;

2. What we need to pass on to our children so that our Christian faith may not die with us;

3. What we must persuade people in our society they need along with the gospel, so that they may adequately understand it and how it may influence their values, life perspectives, and world view. Only by responding to this challenge can we be obedient to the command of our Lord to go into all the world preaching the gospel and making disciples.

Charles Malik once said: "If Christians do not care for the intellectual health of their children and for the fate of their own civilization ... then who is going to care?" The instruction of the Christian church is a desperate need in our day. The mind of the church of Jesus Christ is desperately disordered. No church can be effective to bring clarity and commitment to a world when it is as ignorant of its own basic principles as is our church today. And, unless we engage the church in a mighty program of reeducation, it will be unable to transmit a Christian heritage to its own children or the society around it. As Malik concludes: "This is the greatest task, the historic task, the most needed task, the task—required loud and clear by the Holy Spirit himself—to which evangelicals must humbly address themselves if they would be obedient to Christ in our day."

Kenneth S. Kantzer
Deerfield, Illinois

Chapter 1

DO CHRISTIANS KNOW WHAT THEY NEED TO KNOW?

"Relevant, relevant, relevant," says one youth pastor and master's degree candidate. "That's the key word at my seminary."

And not just at his seminary. American Christians try hard to be relevant—befriending those they want to reach, learning what they care about, then selecting from the gospel what "speaks" to these new friends. Such evangelism and discipling often succeeds. So what's wrong with relevance?

What is wrong is that we have lost our balance. The American church hardly exists as a church any longer. It is hard to be a real church when endless calls for "relevance" have contributed to the fragmentation of believers. And it is hard to be a real church while catering to a society of me-first individuals, buying into the ephemeral and relative values of the culture in order to reach it. By and large, our local churches have forgotten the church universal, the church that through the centuries held to and lived by a shared store of knowledge. They have forgotten (or at least are ignoring) many of the truths Christians hold in common.

That is what we are finding to our alarm—that all too many Christians are forgetting or not learning the basics of the faith. Over the past thirty years of teaching, we have seen every year that more of the young Christians under our care do not know or understand—let alone act on—the faith they claim.

Surprisingly, the call for Americans to return to what they must know—to return to a foundation, to a core—is being loudly proclaimed in the wider culture. In two of 1987's best-selling books, Allan Bloom decried the relativism that has helped cause *The Closing of the American Mind*, and E. D. Hirsch, Jr., listed about five thousand items needed to bolster the nation's waning *Cultural Literacy*.[1] Both are saying that Americans are losing their knowledge of the essentials, the things in common that we must have to keep functioning as a cohesive culture.

The disastrous effects of ignorance

Christian leaders are now sounding similar alarms within the church. Theologian Kenneth Kantzer points out that "every . . . Christian educator I know laments the fact that knowledge about religion, the Bible, and Christianity has fallen off. This is certainly true for the general public, but unfortunately it is true for evangelical Christians as well."[2]

Princeton Theological Seminary's Craig Dykstra agrees. "Such religious illiteracy is not [only] among the unchurched," he writes.

> The church is beset by a devastating lack of religious memory as well—what [was] once bewailed as our "theological amnesia." Many theologians have echoed this diagnosis . . . that "the silence of Scripture in the life of the church" and "the loss of theological tradition" are key factors in and symptoms of a "crisis in Christian identity."[3]

Evidence of the crisis was borne out by a 1988 Gallup poll that found that "many professing believers remain woefully ignorant about basic facts of Christianity."[4]

But is it really that serious? Why can't we just keep on being relevant and evangelizing without expecting Christians to learn a burdensome amount of knowledge about the Christian heritage?

It is because the very act of being relevant almost always means watering down. That is, all too often we select a few "relevant" things from God's revelation—and ignore the rest. That is not what God intends. The Bible *as a whole* is the primary record of what we need to know: God's truth as revealed in Jesus Christ, starting with "In the beginning" and ending with "Amen." When we begin to pick and choose, we are saying we don't have to know and pass on some things. But that was not Paul's course. Faced with what he needed to pass on, he said to Timothy, the spiritual son he was handing his torch to, "And the things thou hast heard of me among many witnesses, the same commit thou to faithful men, who shall be able to teach others also" (2 Tim. 2:2).

The "same." Not "what you decide Rufus or Linus or Apphia need to know," but "the same."

It works like this: Christians hear the Word, they incorporate it into their lives, they find faithful ones (as Paul did Timothy) to commit it to, and they urge the faithful to continue the process. But what if there is a breakdown? What if Christians know and keep only part of the Word, then pass on that part to others who also select only what is most relevant for those *they* find to teach? Just as it happens in the game of gossip, details of the picture get lost and the truth gets garbled.

God assures us in Scripture that a remnant of believers will somehow remain, that the church will not die even if it distorts the gospel. But the church can become dangerously unhealthy when it fragments and loses pieces of the whole gospel counsel. When that occurs, Christians gradually find they cannot fellowship with one another because they don't even talk the same language anymore. Think of a builder who says, "Hand me another brick," but is surrounded by co-workers who don't even know what a brick is. The builder is stymied, the common project is ended. "When communications fail, so do undertakings. (That is the moral of the story of the Tower of Babel.)," comments Hirsch.[5]

This is Christian illiteracy. And it is even more urgent—infinitely more—than cultural illiteracy because it undermines the work of Christ's kingdom.

What Hirsch says of America parallels the situation of the church. It is failing to pass on the "basic information needed to thrive in the modern world." With more than sufficient evidence, he shows that "[o]nly by piling up specific, communally shared information can children learn to participate in complex cooperative activities with other members of their community."[6] In any culture, communication requires not just the ability to read words but also the background of information that is the context for those words. But that all-important context is exactly what Americans—including Christians—are not learning anymore.

Looking ahead

There is no need to rehearse at this point what our youngsters don't know: Test scores are dropping even among the best. Horror stories are twice-told tales, with seventeen-year-olds placing Rome in Canada and not knowing when Columbus discovered America.[7] Ignorance of such fundamentals weakens the individual American's identity as an American and erodes the national sense of community.

Likewise, ignorance of the Christian heritage undermines the Christian identity of individual believers and severely weakens the Christian community—perhaps even to the point that in twenty years, when today's faithful are gone, it could cease to exist at all. There is only one way to turn the tide: We have to recover and pass on the heritage in its fullness.

This process must be ongoing. Not only does the Bible mandate it, the health of the church requires that we find men and women to commit "the same" to. And the very act of committing "the same" will help them become not only knowledgeable, but faithful. We can attest to that experientially. Many of us as young Christians memorized, "Thy word have I hid in mine heart, that I might not sin against thee" (Ps. 119:11), and we know that when the law of our God is in our hearts, our steps will not slip (Ps. 37:31). Our lives have proven this true. We were made more faithful even as we committed the words to memory.

But how can we pass on "the same" if we choose only what seems relevant? And how can even those younger Christians who want to break from the pack become knowledgeable and more faithful if they do not know the basics, and if for them the words—such as *faith*—are meaningless, vague, or twisted?

Again, writes Kenneth Kantzer,

> Every time I hear a radio or television sermon, I find myself wondering how much of this non-Christians understand. What does a reference to "the blood" communicate to them? What meaning do they have for law, sin, grace, regeneration, righteousness, and the basic vocabulary of Christian faith?[8]

But it is not just the non-Christians. In the younger—and older—Christians under our care, we find that all too often, like their pagan peers, they have precious little grasp of the basics. Our concern led us to conclude that it is crucial—now more than ever—to communicate the essential core of the Christian heritage to each succeeding generation of the church.

"Who's this 'Amazing Grace' you keep talking about?"

Our alarm also galvanized us into action. First we tried to determine what Christians should know. From a comprehensive list of terms that exemplify the kinds of knowledge Christians should share, a group of scholars, church leaders, and seminary professors helped us develop a list of terms, dates, names, and concepts; these form the major appendix at the end of the book.

After we had a tentative idea of what Christians should know, we set out to discover what they do—and don't—know through a nationwide survey of over 1,250 *Christianity Today* and *Campus Life* subscribers. The things we learned about the state of Christian knowledge guided us as we wrote the chapters that follow.

Specifically, chapter 2 explores why we need Christian knowledge of greater depth. But recognizing that need then uncovers other problems and questions. Chapter 3 picks up on these. One problem, for example, is determining exactly what constitutes the essential core of our heritage. We cannot know every word of the Bible, of course, so we will have to select. But then how can we avoid being *merely* relevant? How can we know what is truly essential? Chapter 4 tests your Christian knowledge, and with chapter 5 you can compare what you know with the literate Christians we surveyed. Chapter 6 takes up the question, "What *do* Christian young people know?" Chapters 7 and 8 consider what we must do to end the erosion of knowledge—and what might happen if we fail. Scattered throughout the book are boxed sections—written by *Christianity Today* Senior Associate Editor David Neff—that contain background on interesting terms and names.

The time for easy solutions is past, but the time for hope is not. That is why we set out to find what Christians should know—and don't. That is why we cannot keep silent about what needs to be done. What we found has led us to concerns—and convictions—that we want to pass on to you.

Chapter 2

IS CHRISTIAN KNOWLEDGE IMPORTANT?

In spite of the solid reasons for our concern about Christian literacy, some in the church will object, "These terms and concepts can't matter *that* much! Besides, when young people hear words like *invocation* and *sanctification*, their attention will go on *vacation*." Reclaiming Christian knowledge for older Christians, others might add, could be just as hard.

Such issues have to be raised at the outset of our efforts to restore a core of knowledge to the Christian community. As in Jesus' parable about building a tower (Luke 14:28–29), we need to be sure that we know what will be required. And we must ensure that the foundation will be adequate for whatever is built on it. We glanced at our "foundation" in chapter 1; now we want to reveal it, reemphasizing the place for a common core of Christian knowledge. We must also consider objections to the restoration of a common core, and ask what difficulties we face if the restoration is to succeed.

Knowing and belonging

Fellowship—what the Bible calls *koinōnia*—is crucial to the life of Christ's body. One of our strongest needs as humans is to belong, and the church is meant to satisfy that need. But *koinōnia* requires a common body of knowledge and an understanding of common terms. It requires a level of shared understanding that is all too often lacking. Even Christians whose doctrinal differences seem relatively minor have a hard time working together. Too frequently they work against each other rather than against the Enemy.

In the context of the early part of Acts, however, *community* meant that the believers were "united in heart and soul" because their faith had drawn them together (Acts 4:32, NEB). The cause of their "common life in Christ" was what they had come to know about Christ, and the result was unity. Throughout the New Testament, this kind of unity is spoken of in terms of thinking and feeling alike, sharing in the Spirit, displaying the same love for one another, and having the "same turn of mind," as Paul phrases it (Titus 1:4 and Phil. 2:1–2, NEB).

So *koinōnia* is not merely getting together for socials or enjoying the chemistry of personalities that click; it is fellowship in a common faith, meeting with Christian brothers and sisters to pray, study the Word, and find out what God is doing in one another's lives. By this definition, Christians often fall short of community. We get together, but not for true fellowship in our common faith.

And the church, for the most part, is not providing for the deficiencies of those who are not growing much on their own. Some, particularly the young, find Bible study onerous. They could be from the clan of Eutychus (Acts 20:7–12), bored by church meetings to the point of falling asleep. (And they may be in as much danger of falling out of the house of faith as Eutychus was.) They get frustrated: "It's too hard to find things in the Bible. Besides, I don't understand it half the time." Then they just shut their Bibles. That's why they must have community—to encourage them and help them on their way.

But youth and the rest of us will have no community if we have no common knowledge, no shared understandings. We as Christians need this common knowledge so that we can have real dialogue: so that we can read each other's writings, listen to each other's words, and respond to each other in understanding. With common knowledge we can worship, fellowship, work together, and *communicate*, even if we do so across denominational, geographical, racial, and generational lines.

Common knowledge, then, is largely a matter of common language. Language affects the way each of us thinks and feels, so it is a tool or vehicle to use in renewing our individual and common minds. Common language is vital if we are to follow the apostle's command not to let the world "squeeze" us "into its own mold," but instead "remake" our minds according to the gospel (Rom. 12:2, Phillips).

Some linguists hold to the Whorf hypothesis, which suggests that if we have fewer words for something, we cannot think about it as well. For instance, Eskimos have more words for snow than English speakers, because it has so much to do with their lives; the French have more words for the colors between blue and green than we have, and studies show they can identify those shades better. And because English emphasizes verbs, linguists wonder if that makes English speakers even more action oriented.[1]

Similarly, some theologians argue that Adam gained control over the idea of each animal when he named it, and that if we really knew and understood all the names for God and Christ in the Bible, we would know God better.

Common language and common knowledge, in other words, enable us to see and experience the world in a common way. We can think and feel alike because we have a shared context of knowledge within which to do that thinking and feeling. The unity of believers, so evident throughout the Bible, is impossible without a store of facts, stories, songs, and so on, possessed and prized by the church.

Objections to the common core

It is now clear why the church needs a core of common knowledge. But some possible objections remain. So we will treat the rationale for a core by considering objections that could be voiced by some in the church.

Pluralism is a fact of life, and the diversity it fosters is actually a benefit. We agree that pluralism has its place. No doubt each generation should emphasize certain aspects of Christianity, some that it sees were ignored in the previous generation. So in searching for and promoting a common core of knowledge, we do not deny that pluralism exists. But it must be pluralism within the light of certain absolutes, within the framework of unchanging truths reflected and passed on in the common core. Thus we follow the old dictum that emphases change, but absolutes don't.

That is why we must remember, as C. S. Lewis so often pointed out, that each generation has both its blind spots and its correct perceptions.[2] And that is why we need history and the other liberal arts more than we may think, for they give us perspective and keep us from seeing the trends of our day as the last word. In a survey of 255 pastors in nineteen denominations, one of the most significant findings was the high correlation between pastors who dropped out of ministry and who also had a narrow education (only in Bible). When the going got tough, they lacked the perspective their liberal arts–trained colleagues had that might have enabled them to stay with their call.[3]

One of the most frightening images of the twentieth century is Jim Jones and his suicidal Guyana cult. Behind the chair that served as Jones's throne was a sign quoting the philosopher Santayana: "Those who cannot remember the past are condemned to repeat it." Ironically, Jones's followers were unable to benefit from history. They drank poisoned Kool-Aid because they hadn't learned from the past to recognize and turn away from a demagogue.

Isaac Newton, a Christian who understood history, explained, "If I have seen further than you . . . it is by standing upon the shoulders of Giants." This shows he knew, well enough to echo, the teaching of Saint Bernard of Clairvaux about the apostles and early church fathers: "We are like dwarfs on the shoulders of giants but as dwarfs we are able to see farther than others only as long as we do not climb down from the giant shoulders."[4]

If we don't know our Christian heritage well enough to travel in it as Newton did, then we are doomed to walk into the same errors over again, to fall short of the rich spiritual life these pathfinders can show us, or to spend time reinventing priorities from year to year.

All this talk about common knowledge sounds like overintellectualizing to me. In real *faith,* loving *is central, not knowing; the heart is what matters, not the head.* With this objection as with the preceding one, we can begin by agreeing. Loving *is* central; it is the law of Christ (James 2:8; Gal. 6:2). As we have noted, *koinōnia* is having "the same love for one another" (Phil. 2:2, NEB). In fact, Paul sets the priority of love first (1 Cor. 8:1; 14:1). So we aren't trying to place knowledge above love. But we must have *both* loving and knowing; each needs to be complemented by the other.

To put it another way, we want to join minds with hearts. That is one reason American Christians since the Puritans have emphasized Christian education in churches and schools. The words we think and talk with, and that others use to talk to us, affect how we feel and how we think. It is a cycle.

With so much to know about the faith, we'll get overwhelmed if we try to sort out what belongs to the core. We agree the task will be hard. But then, if God had wanted for his followers only a stripped-down gospel tract, the Bible wouldn't have sixty-six books. The flip side of this concern is that we may fail to avail ourselves of all the riches God has given us.

To answer the objection more directly, however, we can point out that the core need not be as large as one might think—even after two millennia of Christian history. The list we have compiled for this book, for instance, includes about eighteen hundred terms and phrases, which many Christians have agreed they need to know to grow in and pass on the faith.

Of course, the eighteen hundred items on our list are open to debate. And that brings up another aspect of the objection that isolating a core is an impossible task. Given the diversity and even contradictions among church denominations and organizations, how can there be consensus on the core? The differences are daunting, but there are living indications that Christians from divergent backgrounds can achieve genuine consensus. An example is Taizé, a monastic community in France. Without waffling on essentials, Taizé is trying to broaden what different Christian groups can harmonize on. The lay brothers there—Roman Catholic, Orthodox, Protestant—view theirs as a mission to the church, a ministry of reconciliation for the whole body. For them, Christ is the commonality. They are not aiming for a single denomination but for an approach to faith that allows all Christians to work together across denominational lines.[5]

Ventures like Taizé show us that consensus takes courage. The contemporary church needs great courage and, with it, great faith—faith that God is not the "author of confusion" (1 Cor. 14:33). His hard-sought, hard-won truth will be one.

The task would be easier, of course, if the core were limited to the Bible. And the Bible is certainly central—the core of the core, so to speak. But, as we have noted, history lends perspective; we are impoverished if we do not avail ourselves of the insights of Christian history since the close of the Canon. In addition, community thrives on its common art, images, and music. To ignore these is again to impoverish ourselves. A list of terms broader than the Bible takes into account the familiar premise, "All truth is God's truth."

Yet another reason for including what is outside the Bible is that language changes. Words, even biblical words, change through time. The New Testament, as we know, was not written in the old-fashioned classical Greek—it was the current street Greek, or *koinē*. And just as the New Testament was current, modern Christians need to keep up with certain changes (which is a case for relevance of a sort).

One example of what we mean is the biblical phrase "born again." Not so long ago it simply meant conversion to Christ. As the Lord told Nicodemus, "You must be born again" (John 3:7, NKJV). But now, it has taken on less savory associations in the national mind. So the *Doublespeak Dictionary* comments in defining the phrase, "We should remember that to be born again one must previously have been dead. And the lingering odor of that former state is difficult to ignore."[6]

So we can work out by consensus what we must pass on, using the Bible as a base and guide, but recognizing as well that our community depends on commonality. This includes cognitive knowledge (such as history and theology) and affective knowledge (such as literature and music), and it includes the changing connotations of language (such as "born again").

A list of core knowledge is artificial and rigid. Memorizing a few hundred terms doesn't make someone a committed Christian. Obviously, we do not see a common core as a cure-all for every ailment of the contemporary church. More than intellectual knowledge is needed, and certainly more than knowledge of the relatively few terms and phrases on our list. Yet a core list is at least a place to start. It is by no means the tree of all knowledge; rather, it is a taste of the abundance of the fruit passed down to us.

And, surprising as it may seem to a society that still is suspicious of the need to master facts and names and dates, memorization is coming back into style. James Moffett is one current educator who praises it. Although he has championed for years the "new" learning, utilizing learning centers and small groups, he also now endorses the poet who said that learning poetry "by heart" truly means it is doing something in our hearts.[7] That is, the learning affects us, even (or especially) if it is word for word.

Memorization is most meaningful when what is memorized is put into a context. That is another reason we should encourage teachers and parents to have children learn with their hearts as well as their minds. They could even learn what is on our core list if it is integrated into their everyday experiences. When teachers and parents emphasize memorizing in context, children build a reservoir they can draw from later. And no doubt those children are the base for future Christian literacy.

I can see how some of the core could be interesting to know, but what does it have to do with my life? I don't see a direct application. Our reply is that sometimes we understand only later how what is being taught applies to our lives, just as the purpose of Noah's ark became all too clear to those who formerly mocked Noah for building a boat in a land without rain. An illustration comes from a student who complained that he was wasting his time learning all about existentialism. But later, he tells us, he understood that was not so. The very next week, after that part of the class was completed, he found himself having to use what he had learned to help a suicidal woman. She had bought into existentialism, but because of his background he was able to discuss the philosophy with her and show her Christ is the answer to even so profound a despair.

The principle is summarized in the words of a veteran teacher we know. As she says when she is trying to teach a key concept: "I think I know what you need to know." So also God will be the great Integrator for us—bringing to our minds later what we need out of the compartments we threw it into long ago, when we did not see the point (note Jesus' words in John 14:26 that the Spirit will "bring to your remembrance all that I have said to you").

Another friend can relate to that. The spiritual encounters that stand out the most from his teen years came in his all-night talks with his uncle, who also was his pastor. As it would begin to get light, his uncle would ask, "Do you understand what Uncle has been saying to you?"

He would reply, "Yes, I understand."

"No, you don't," his uncle would respond, "but someday you will, and you will remember that Uncle told you this."

And he has—he has been able in later life to draw that knowledge from those previously unused compartments. The usefulness of the knowledge contained there, in the vast reservoir of the biblical and Christian heritage, has been proven over and over again by the millions of saints before us, who have drawn from it, even though sometimes they did not know at first what particular thirst it would satisfy.

New Christians, or prospects for conversion, will be frightened off by an intimidating core of knowledge. No one is proposing that knowledge of the core be made a prerequisite to entering the faith. So the real question is, *How long will these new believers be beginners?* Aren't they in the same state the writer to the Hebrews chided his hearers for—they are only milk drinkers, not meat eaters? "Anyone who lives on milk, being an infant, does not know what is right" (Heb. 5:13, NEB). He "is unskilled in the word of righteousness, for he is a babe" (Heb. 5:13, NKJV).

In any endeavor we care about, it will not long satisfy us to remain unskilled. Neither the tennis player nor her coaches would be happy if she didn't reach her full potential, if she remained uncoordinated and clumsy. So also, the spiritual "babes" under our care need to be trained and taught, given skills, and brought to where they can digest meat. Otherwise, Christian illiteracy makes Christians fall guys for cults and for the sticky-sweet covering of New Age reason ing. The Bible warns over and over about being untaught, unstable, naïve, ignorant, and foolish.

Some people who know the most about the faith live wretched lives. Knowledge doesn't necessarily make us spiritually or psychologically healthy. We too can think of people who possess a great deal of knowledge but live immorally. And we don't deny that some people, burdened with guilt, *already* memorize Scripture, pray at length, and faithfully attend church. Do they really need exhortations to study more—and harder?

In reply, we again emphasize that knowledge is not a panacea or guarantee. But neither is it just a Band-Aid. We believe it is a central part of living a moral life or being healed of psychological wounds.

"So we're approaching Armageddon. It's not the end of the world."

After all, people cannot live morally unless they know what is the moral way to live. And the person struggling with, say, low self-esteem, will benefit greatly from a correct understanding of grace—that God loves us and deems us valuable whatever our shortcomings.

The real key is how knowledge is incorporated into our lives. Discipleship means letting knowledge of the faith shape and form us in new and stretching ways. Only as Christians relate to other knowledgeable Christians will they discover how to live out the Word they learn.

In chapter 1 we mentioned the Paul-to-Timothy discipling process. In that process the things the student learned were not only *taught* by word, but also *caught* by life. Paul had Timothy go everywhere with him, so Timothy learned his mentor's style. We know a pastoral ministries professor who tries to do this by taking his students out to help him on evangelistic crusades. In this way knowledge is "gained by association" before it is "understood by explanation."[8]

A different kind of relevance

We do not mean to dismiss relevance out of hand. What we seek is a relevance in perspective, set into the context of a body of knowledge that helps us appreciate who we are by informing us where we came from. In other words, we favor a balanced relevance.

Balanced relevance means always building on the foundations of the faith. It means not stopping at milk when we should be moving on to meat. It means not picking and choosing what I like for myself, even if that has become the American way. It means not getting blindly caught up in whatever is trendy. Balanced relevance insists on not only what seems best for today, but also what Christians have found most important during the past two thousand years, like Genesis 1:1, *Pilgrim's Progress,* or "A Mighty Fortress Is Our God."

Balanced relevance requires looking beyond short-term, apparent success—beyond what "works." In a misguided zeal for uncritical relevance, Christians have increasingly accommodated to the culture. But accommodation has not worked. Christians have accommodated so much that the world is not only not attracted to the church, it only despises the church.

Paul offers a counterexample. He certainly was relevant, but in a balanced fashion. He communicated to people in their circumstances (1 Cor. 9:19–23), but he never watered down the faith. He maintained and passed on a clear core. So must we. Otherwise we make relevance more important than our witness to the kingdom.

It is tempting, to be sure, to offer painless, short-term answers to the fragmentation we see everywhere around us. Our culture, enamored of instant gratification, expects that. Instead, we are pleading for believers to unite in looking back to where the church has been and looking ahead to where it is going. That is the only way to avoid a reactionary response to the crisis.

All that we have said leads us to two projections. First, if we continue to let the common Christian core of knowledge erode, the work of the kingdom will be undermined. Yes, there is the scriptural promise that even the gates of hell will not prevail against the church (Matt. 16:18), but nothing guarantees that the church will not grow sicker and sicker. And nothing guarantees that the church in a particular location, even that of an entire nation, won't face extinction. (The church at Ephesus was threatened with the removal of its light [Rev. 2:5].) The American church is not assured of institutional immortality.

But the second projection offers hope. The church can be built by Christians who are tied together by knowing the core that has been passed down by faithful people from generation to generation. The power of knowledge shared in common is evident in the case of two church groups working together in inner-city ministries. They were so separated by differences—age, economics, denomination, race—that they weren't even aware of each other. But in time they discovered a profound common denominator: They were both carrying out God's commands to feed the hungry in the name of Christ. When they saw that, they concluded, "This is ridiculous; why haven't we been working together?"

This may be one small commonality, a mere thread. But put together enough of them, and they will form a cable on which to hang a bridge that Christians can walk across to be together, to be in community, to be one.

Chapter 3

HOW CAN WE FIND WHAT IS ESSENTIAL?

In explaining the value of Christian knowledge, we said in chapter 2 that Christians need to know the Bible in order to have a sound foundation for faith and life, know Christian history and other liberal arts in order to keep perspective and wholeness, and know something about theology and changing language in order to achieve balanced relevance. Now we elaborate on why these three categories of knowledge are important, and how we eventually arrived at our core list.

Christians will have no difficulty agreeing that the Bible is at the center of what we all need to know. We can also agree that we must begin with the truth of God as revealed in Jesus Christ, and, further, that at the center of Jesus' story is his crucifixion and resurrection. The general agreement expands yet wider, to such traditional affirmations as the Apostles' Creed (recited often by Roman Catholics, Lutherans, Presbyterians, Methodists, and many other Christians). Common heritage does not end there, either. We can move ahead to Christian history, and to books and songs that have proven themselves by lasting long and well. Finally comes the more difficult task of deciding what current issues and concerns should be included in the core. It will help to examine each of these dimensions in detail.

At the core of the core: The Bible

The value of a core of knowledge—to aid us in interpreting and appropriating the rest—is itself exemplified in Scripture. One New Testament inquirer, wanting to get at the core, asked Jesus what was most important. Apparently considering the question legitimate, Jesus answered that there are two foremost commandments: loving God and loving your neighbor (Luke 10:27). And Jesus and the apostles often presented the saving gospel in concise form, as in the best known of all Bible references, John 3:16, or as in Romans 10:9 and 1 Corinthians 15:3–6. So, since the time of Christ's ministry, his followers have passed on the central truth that salvation comes through believing in him as the Son of God and confessing his name.

Of the apostles, Paul modeled this focus most often: He determined to know nothing among the Corinthians except "Jesus Christ and him crucified" (1 Cor. 2:2). Following Paul's lead is a traditional way to select what gospel to share—"fix[ing] our thoughts" on Christ (Heb. 3:1, NIV) and following the "red line" pointing to redemption throughout Scripture.[1] The same method is practiced by the Master, most explicitly in his conversation with the two disciples on the way to Emmaus: "How dull you are! . . . How slow to believe all that the prophets said!" Then the Lord began with Moses and moved through all the prophets, explaining as he went the passages that spoke of him (Luke 24:13–35, NEB).

The witness of Jesus and Paul was followed by the entire New Testament church. The most memorable term for that church, *koinōnia*, as we have said, can mean agreement and consensus. The modern tendency may be to think of this "one accord" as mystical and perhaps mystifying. But the record shows that the consensus was no nebulous feeling or vague affection. Acts 15 indicates how the young church reaffirmed what it believed and decided what was relevant to the culture (decreeing that Gentile believers need not adopt all the customs of Judaism).

But of course the Bible also charges us with knowing more than the essential gospel. We are called to know both the milk and the meat of the Word. For example, the writer to the Hebrews joins in identifying the "foundations" or "rudiments of Christianity": "faith in God and . . . repentance from the deadness of our former ways, . . . instruction about cleansing rites and the laying-on-of-hands, about the resurrection of the dead and eternal judgement" (Heb. 6:1–2, NEB).

The purpose of that passage is not to emphasize the simple gospel but instead to urge the readers to "stop discussing the rudiments" in order to "advance towards maturity." In fact, the writer has just rebuked them: "For . . . though by this time you ought to be teachers, you need someone to teach you the ABC of God's oracles over again; it has come to this, that you need milk instead of solid food. . . . But grown men can take solid food; their perceptions are trained by long use to discriminate between good and evil" (Heb. 5:11–14, NEB).

Paul called the Corinthian church to account for the same failure. He said that they, being carnal, could not yet bear the meat of the Word but only the milk he was having to feed them (1 Cor. 3:2). There is other evidence that Paul set priorities on both these levels, the immediate "good news" and a wider core. He never stopped his ministry, which he had "received of the Lord Jesus, to testify the gospel of the grace of God," as he said to the Ephesian elders in what he assumed were his final words to them. But he also knew he was accountable to God for giving them more than milk, since he said: "I am pure from the blood of all men. For I have not shunned to declare unto you *all* the counsel of God" (Acts 20:24–27).

How then shall we decide what knowledge is vital and how best to convey it? Once again, we look to Christ for our answer and model. Jesus took the Passover celebration, observed for countless generations in Israel, and expanded it to teach the gospel—participation in his sacrifice of body and blood (Exod. 12:1–11; John 13:1; 1 Cor. 5:7; 11:23–26). In addition to content, this new covenant "Passover" implies a model method: It contains both propositional and metaphorical truth about the paschal Lamb of God "who takes away the sin of the world" (John 1:29).

Not Quite English

Biblical words that lose something in the translation.

Because the first Christians spoke Aramaic and Greek, Christians today continue to speak in foreign words and phrases. Here are some of the most common:

Abba. In Mark 14:36, Jesus is quoted as saying, "Abba, Father, all things are possible to thee," as he prayed in the Garden of Gethsemane. The Aramaic *Abba* means "father" in the way that *Daddy* or *Papa* mean "father." One of Jesus' most distinctive contributions to our understanding of God was this intimate cry of the child, "Abba!" And it seems that the early Christians followed Jesus' example by using the word to address God in prayer. In Romans 8:15, Paul says it is the Spirit of God who allows us to "cry, Abba, Father"; and in Galatians 4:6, Paul says that "God has sent the Spirit of his Son into our hearts, crying, 'Abba! Father!' "

agape. Paul wrote a beautiful hymn of unselfish Christian love, or *agapē,* in 1 Corinthians 13. But this unusual Greek word for "love" was made famous by two modern Christian writers: the literary scholar C. S. Lewis in *The Four Loves* and Lutheran bishop and biblical scholar Anders Nygren in *Agape and Eros*. Nygren contended that Paul took a rarely used word for love in order to avoid confusion with the more common Greek words *eros* and *philia*, sexual love and friendly affection. Then Paul infused the word with meaning drawn from the self-sacrificing love of Christ. Early Christians were so fond of this word that they not only applied it to the virtue they emulated, but to the shared meal in which they celebrated their spiritual unity. Such a "love feast" was called an *agapē.*

alleluia (hallelujah). One of the best-loved words in the Christian vocabulary, it is also perhaps the most spoken and sung. There is no mystery as to what it means: The Hebrew *halelu* is the imperative "Praise!" and the final syllable (*jah*) is a shortened form of God's sacred name *Yahweh* (translated as *Jehovah* in the KJV).

amen. The word appears thirty times in the Old Testament and 150 times in the New. Most Christians say it several times a day. It is a Hebrew word of affirmation: *So be it. Verily.* Jesus used it quite a lot. His stern formula for introducing his sayings, "Verily, verily, I say unto you," used this word twice: "Amen, amen, I tell you," some translations say. But Jesus used this common word in an unusual way. In his day, *amēn* was something other people said to show their agreement with what you had just said, to bind themselves to your oath or to agree with your prayer. From extant records it seems that Jesus was unique in saying *amēn* to his own words, and in prefacing his own pronouncements with these words of utter certainty. Since Jesus' time Christians followed Jewish practice in joining in prayers of their worship leaders by uttering the *amēn*. And in still later time, they appended it to their own prayers as an affirmation. In Revelation 3:14, Christ is revealed as the true *amēn* and as "the faithful and true witness." He is the word of certainty behind all our prayers and hopes.

anathema. This word is used in the most common Greek translation of the Old Testament to translate *cherem*, the Hebrew word that described the cities, peoples, and cattle that God commanded the Israelites to destroy. It also referred to holy things that were God's alone. But in the New Testament and in modern English it refers to people who are cursed and doomed to destruction. Thus Paul wrote in Galatians 1:8 that if anyone should preach a different gospel than the one he had preached, "let him be *anathema*."

jot and tittle. Jesus said, "Until heaven and earth pass away, not a jot, not a tittle, will pass from the law until all is accomplished" (Matt. 5:18). Most Christians know that Jesus was saying the law was of lasting value. Few Christians know what a jot or a tittle is. The "jot" stands for the smallest Hebrew letter (the *yodh)* or the smallest Greek letter (the *iota)*. The word *tittle* means "horn" and refers to a small decorative flourish on any of several Hebrew letters. In other words, "Not the smallest letter, not even a decorative flourish will pass from the law until all is accomplished." Or as E. J. Goodspeed has it, "Not one dotting of an *i* nor crossing of a *t*."

koinonia. Derived from the Greek word for things that are held in common, *koinōnia* refers to the communion, the brotherly bond, that exists among people who have something important in common. In Acts, it is used to describe the common worship life of the early church. But when Paul adopted the term it took on a special meaning: not a human society, but the relation of faith to Christ. Thus we have Paul's typical phrases "the fellowship of his Son" and "the fellowship of the Holy Spirit." Modern Christians tend to use the word much more like the author of 1 John: the fellowship in the faith that Christians share because of their belief in the apostolic teaching, their common walking in the light, and the cleansing blood of Jesus.

maranatha. An Aramaic word found only in 1 Corinthians 16:22, *maranatha* either means, "Our Lord has come," or "Our Lord, come!" Other early Christian literature (ca. 100) uses the word in prayers connected to the Lord's Supper. It seems to be an ejaculatory prayer like the cry *Abba!* (q.v.)—a heart-felt plea for the Lord to come in judgment and set right all that is wrong with this world.

Propositions—clear, literal statements and commands—here combine with metaphors, truths that are figuratively stated. Propositions—"In the beginning God created the heavens and the earth," or "Thou shalt not kill"—usually form the basis of systematic theologies and ethical systems. On the other hand, metaphors—"The Lord is my shepherd," or "Blessed is the man that walketh not in the counsel of the ungodly"—speak to the heart, to comfort or convict. The Passover—and our commemoration of the Lord's Supper—incorporates both kinds of truth into lives, involving our emotions (and bodies) as well as our minds as we act out the truth.

Actually, most of what Jesus said was couched in the graphic, figurative language we believe we must include for balanced knowledge—language that can puzzle and still pack power. The impact of a metaphor like swallowing a camel or a story like the parable of the prodigal son forces us to remember and meditate on what we have heard—bringing it back up again later to chew on much as a cow chews on her cud. Award-winning writer Madeleine L'Engle understands how that works, testifying from her own life what stories—like those of Jesus—really mean: "I knew from an early age that I had very difficult questions about the universe and life: . . . What's life about? Does it matter? Does our life have any meaning or answers? . . . [Y]ou can't answer those questions except in stories."[2]

Christians, then, need to know propositions such as those found in Paul's explication of faith and works in Romans 4–6, or in his hymn of praise and prayer in Ephesians 1 that almost flies above the bounds of language. But they also need to know, as L'Engle recognizes, the stories and parables and metaphors that Jesus favored, as well as the stories and psalms and poetry from the rest of the Bible. That is why we searched through more than biblical propositions as we worked on our list. That is why the core list includes the central terms of the biblical story and its retellings, terms that appeal to the senses and the imagination as well as to the mind. "We need and value," says Leland Ryken, "all the ways in which we take in and 'know' the truth."[3]

Adding tradition

All this shows what we mean by having the Bible, as well as Christ's and Paul's approaches to interpreting it, demonstrate the way for us as we look for the Christian core. Scripture, of course, can help us know what to appropriate as we move beyond it into postcanonical Christian tradition. Here we are after what Christians through the ages have deemed central. Apologist C. S. Lewis followed a similar approach in trying to discern what was basic to Christianity. "Ever since I became a Christian I have thought that the best, perhaps the only, service I could do for my unbelieving neighbours was to explain and defend the belief that has been common to nearly all Christians at all times . . . what [seventeenth-century English clergyman Richard] Baxter calls 'mere' Christianity."[4]

We offer as central, too, classics from literature, which many faithful, literate Christians continue to have at least a nodding acquaintance with, even if they have not read them, such as Augustine's *Confessions*, Dante's *Inferno*, à Kempis's *Of the Imitation of Christ*, Aquinas's *Summa Theologica*, Bunyan's *Pilgrim's Progress*, and Milton's *Paradise Lost*. If past Christians could speak, they would surely advise us to rebuild what has been lost so that more of us would at least know *about* the classics. They would see them as solid food. And present-day Christians who know them have found them precious and valuable for their spiritual journeys.

Tradition also includes church history. So many events and Christians from times past are more vital in their continuing influence than their current name recognition would suggest. Jonathan Edwards is a good example. If Americans know his name at all, it is merely to link him with the fearful sermon "Sinners in the Hands of an Angry God." His greater legacy is the nation's predisposition to revival preaching—seen even today in the crusade evangelism of Billy Graham and Luis Palau. All this can be traced back to the mid-eighteenth century Great Awakening, during which Edwards preached, and to which he devoted his considerable intellectual weight.

But not knowing church history goes deeper than not appreciating our Christian roots. As we have noted, it also means repeating the errors of the past. In 1988, small groups of Christians around the country were caught up in expecting the Rapture in mid-September—although Scripture warns against such presumption, and a number of sects in the past have wrongly set such dates.[5] If they had known their history, these Christians would have been forewarned and could have avoided their error. We make a case, then, for including church history in what Christians need to know.

Currency and the core

What about current issues that relate to the biblical and traditional core? How can we decide what to include here? "We are in Christ—and also in this age," Augustine said.[6] The corollary is that Christians need to know something about the age in which they live. Jesus himself integrated current events into a spiritual context when he explained the eternal meaning of deaths caused by a falling tower and by Pilate's massacre of some Galileans (Luke 13:1–5).

Present-day leaders who are teaching us how to contextualize our witness often advise following the Pauline pattern of becoming all things to all people (1 Cor. 9:22). Biblical scholar Alan Johnson says,

> [C]ommunication has to be contextually oriented. We learn by the paradigm of the New Testament itself. Each of the four Gospels has a different ethnic contextualization. And as the gospel went out of the Palestinian Jewish culture into other parts of the world, certain kinds of terminology were dropped because they did not have coinage in these communities.[7]

Paul put it simply in 1 Corinthians 9:20: "To the Jews I became as a Jew."

We can contextualize our own witness only if we know what "all people" care about: pollution, drugs, the threat of war, violence in the streets, family breakdown. But how much of such current concern is part of what Christians need to know? And how do we still take care not to substitute temporal values for eternal ones?

In devising our core list, we have assumed that knowledge of contemporary affairs is the easiest to gain. After all, we do live in this age. Television, radio, the newspapers, and other mass media bombard us with the concerns and fixations of the day. So, though knowledge of current events is important, our core list emphasizes traditional, less ephemeral knowledge. And while the main subject of this book is not consensus on current issues, we would suggest that such agreement is not even thinkable unless Christians first attend to the common core inherited from those who have gone before us. To expand on our line of reasoning: Christians are living in an increasingly alien culture. That means our witness is increasingly cross cultural. If you don't have a firm hold on what you believe, how can you put what you believe into the terms of other people's culture? How can you help them recognize the "eternity" that God has put "in their hearts" if you are not familiar with his eternal truths (Eccles. 3:11)? Or, to put it another way, how can you recognize something as an "unfocused gleam of divine truth" if you don't know what the focused truth is?[8]

We have shown that the crux of what we need to know is the truth of God as revealed in Jesus Christ, and that Christians have set biblical priorities—first the gospel, then the meat of the Word. They have operated out of some things in common (such as the Apostles' Creed, classic Christian writings, church history). They want to find some measure of agreement on current issues (such as politics or pollution). And they experience in common both propositional and

"My wife just left me, I lost my job, and my spirits have hit bottom! Pastor, you've got to help me! What's the difference between pre-, post-, and amillennialism?"

metaphorical truth. That is what we see as the core.

The nitty-gritty of arriving at the core

This background provides a general sense of how we approached the construction of a core list. But how did we arrive at the final list?

Our first step was a brainstorming and screening process, consulting concordances and experts, reading the Bible through, carrying notebooks everywhere we went to record what Christians say. By those methods we compiled a preliminary list of over three thousand terms. Next, we refined the list with the help of just under a hundred selected Christians, both young and old, who ranked each item from *most important* to *least important*. Then *Christianity Today* Resource Scholars and editors provided input. At that point the list was reduced to 1,031 representative terms, a size manageable for a mail-in survey.

That survey of almost thirteen hundred Christians—some from Christian campuses, others from selected youth groups and churches, and most from readers of *Campus Life* and *Christianity Today*—ranked terms by how well respondents knew them. The survey responses provided a base for our chapters about what literate Christians know (chap. 5) and what young Christians know (chap. 6). The surveys were helpful, too, in fine tuning the final core list that appears as an appendix at the end of the book.

An obvious question would be, "But even if we could agree on the terms you have settled on, what good would that be without common meanings to the terms?" In the long run, in order to pass on the core to faithful people, we would require agreed-upon meanings for each key term. But there can be only one step taken at a time. Just knowing terms—which is the first step, the one we are recommending here—will move us toward better communication and therefore more unity within the body. The next chapter, a Christian knowledge self-test, lets you find out what you already know—and what you may need to learn—for us to start reclaiming consensus.

Chapter 4

WHAT DO YOU KNOW? TEST YOURSELF

Quick. Who wrote 1 Corinthians? What does it mean to fall into the Slough of Despond? Who was Roger Williams?

Can you answer questions like these? An increasing number of Christians can't.

Or do you know more than you think you know? To help you find out, we have put together sixteen short tests of Christian knowledge—some easy, some more difficult—about people, places, Bible verses, and writings. Based on the list of terms in the appendix, they provide a sample of the types of knowledge you will find there.

Answers are given in the endnotes for chapter 4. With a little boning up, you will amaze yourself (and your friends) with your knowledge. Don't try to digest all the tests at once. But this first test should whet your appetite for more. Many Christians we've tested scored 100 percent on it.

Test 1: Common Bible Sayings I

1. Am I my brother's ________?
2. Daniel in the ________ den
3. Do unto ________ as you would have them do unto you.
4. Eat, drink, and be merry, for tomorrow we ________.
5. a friend that sticks closer than a ________
6. God so loved the ________ that he gave his only begotten son.
7. I am the ________, the truth, and the life.
8. In my Father's ________ are many mansions.
9. land flowing with milk and ________
10. Lay up for yourselves ________ in heaven, where neither moth nor rust doth corrupt nor thieves break through and steal.
11. ________ is the substance of things hoped for, the evidence of things not seen.
12. no ________ in the inn
13. Now abideth faith, hope, ________, these three; but the greatest of these is ________.
14. Suffer the little ________ to come unto me, and forbid them not.
15. Turn the ________ cheek.
16. Walk by ________, not by sight.
17. ________ up a child in the way he should go, and when he is old, he will not depart from it.
18. All we like ________ have gone astray.
19. Be ye ________ of the word, and not hearers only.
20. Create in me a clean ________, O God.

One Sunday school class averaged 91 percent on the test that follows. However, less than half of one group of church leaders knew the Great Commission—and two of them thought Jimmy Carter originated the term *born again*.

Test 2: About the Bible

1. Where did the term *born again* originate?
2. What books of the Bible are referred to as the "Gospels"?

3. What is the total number of books found in the Bible?
4. Name the three persons of the Trinity.
5. What is the shortest verse in the Bible?
6. What is the "Golden Rule"?
7. What book of the Bible has the greatest number of chapters?
8. Is the Book of Hezekiah found in the Old or New Testament?
9. What are the first five books of the Old Testament called as a group?
10. Tell in your own words what the "Great Commission" is.

Have you made the Bible the habit of your life? If so, this next test—it's all in the Bible—will be duck soup for you.

Test 3: In the Bible

1–4. Name the first four books of the New Testament.
5. In what book of the Bible is the Christmas story found, the version familiar to most people?
6. What is another well-known name for "the Evil One"?
7. In the Old Testament, who was turned into a pillar of salt?
8–12. Name the first five books of the Old Testament.
13. Who was Joseph's younger brother (the youngest son of Jacob)?
14. What was the name of the daily food God provided as Moses led his people through the wilderness?
15. Who was the first king of Israel?
16. What town is known as the "City of David"?
17. Name the wicked queen who wanted to kill Elijah.
18. Jesus said that the greatest commandment is "Thou shalt love the Lord thy God with all thy heart, . . . soul, . . . mind." What did he say the *second* greatest command is?
19. Who was the man who wrestled with an angel at Peniel?
20. What body of water parted for Moses?

People are fascinated by people. The ones on the following test would all have been in the *People* magazine of their day, but they are not daily fodder for the media now.

Test 4: People

___ 1. Absalom	A. A military leader of Israel
___ 2. John Wycliffe	B. Archbishop of Canterbury who was murdered in that cathedral
___ 3. Matthias	C. Brothcr of Moses
___ 4. Ahab	D. Important Old Testament prophet
___ 5. John Wesley	E. Minister who founded an American colony
___ 6. Barnabas	F. Had a daughter healed by Jesus
___ 7. Gideon	G. Wicked king of Israel
___ 8. C. S. Lewis	H. Famous Bible translator
___ 9. Jairus	I. Accompanied Paul on missionary journey
___ 10. Hezekiah	J. David's son
___ 11. Roger Williams	K. Wrote *Mere Christianity*
___ 12. Stephen	L. Was chosen to replace Judas Iscariot
___ 13. Samuel	M. Good king of Judah
___ 14. Thomas Becket	N. Founder of the Methodist Church
___ 15. Aaron	O. The first Christian martyr

Not all Christian knowledge is as easy as pie. Some will find certain of the following terms and phrases confusing. (One group who averaged scores of 88 percent and above on other tests dropped to 70 percent here.)

Test 5: Terms and Phrases

___ 1. Divine Comedy: (A) Michael Landon TV series "Highway to Heaven" (B) how God laughs in derision at arrogant nations as in Psalm 2 (C) Dante's Italian epic of heaven and hell

___ 2. Day of the Lord: (A) Second Coming (B) Sunday (C) Easter (D) Ascension Day

___ 3. Eternal security: (A) Eternity is sure to come (B) One cannot become unsaved (C) Heaven will last forever (D) It refers to Elijah's being taken up in a chariot

___ 4. "Nothing new under the sun . . .": (A) Solomon (B) David (C) Isaiah (D) Elijah

___ 5. Epistle: (A) one of the twelve disciples (B) an ancient weapon (C) a letter (D) a battle

___ 6. Farthing: (A) a small coin (B) a type of dove (C) a little lake (D) a confession

___ 7. Lectionary: (A) the third section of a Mass (B) a series of sermons (C) a set of Scripture readings for the year (D) the rulers in a Greek Orthodox Church

___ 8. "I believe in God the Father Almighty . . .": (A) Gloria Patri (B) Pope John XXIII (C) Apostles' Creed (D) Pentateuch

___ 9. *Sanctum sanctorum*: (A) believers set aside for God's work (B) persons who have been sanctified and do not sin (C) the process of forgiveness following confession (D) the innermost room in the Jewish temple

___ 10. Scopes trial: (A) the Roman trial of the apostle Andrew (B) questioned the authenticity of the Apostles' Creed (C) argument over creation versus evolution (D) disagreement between the heads of the Anglican and Catholic churches

___ 11. Glossolalia: (A) the shiny surface on certain religious paintings (B) euphoric state of mind following baptism (C) miraculous healing (D) speaking in tongues

___ 12. "Blessed are the merciful . . . ": (A) Beatitudes (B) parables (C) Book of James (D) Nicene Creed

___ 13. "Hallowed be thy name. Thy kingdom come. . . .": (A) Psalm 23 (B) Matthew 6:9 (C) John 5:2 (D) Acts 16:31

___ 14. Tithe: (A) the altar where gifts were laid (B) instrument of worship used by the Levites (C) the rope used to lead a donkey (D) a part of one's income given to God

___ 15. "Surely he hath borne our griefs . . .": (A) Brahms's *Requiem* (B) Book of Isaiah (C) the Doxology (D) prophecy of Joel

___ 16. Being "born again": (A) justification (B) sanctification (C) regeneration (D) glorification

___ 17. The study of Christ's second coming and the end times: (A) eschatology (B) omnipotence (C) hermeneutics (D) ascension

___ 18. Another name for the Ten Commandments: (A) denomination (B) decadence (C) decameter (D) decalogue

___ 19. Eucharist: (A) baptism (B) sanctification (C) Lord's Supper (D) ecumenical

___ 20. The main part of the church where the people sit: (A) narthex (B) transept (C) nave (D) reredos

The next test will be, like a cup of cold water, a refreshing change of pace for those who find the following words familiar, like the high proportion of Christians we tested who scored 100 percent.

Test 6: Common Bible Sayings II

1. Death, where is thy ________?
2. Don't hide your ________ under a bushel.
3. Gold, frankincense, and ________.
4. I am come that they might have ________ and that they might have it more abundantly.
5. I am the light of the ________.
6. If ________ be for us, who can be against us?
7. If ye love me, ________ my commandments.
8. In the ________ God created the heavens and the earth.
9. The just shall live by ________.
10. Lead us not into ________, but deliver us from evil.
11. Man shall not live by ________ alone, but by every word of God.
12. A new commandment I give unto you, that ye ________ one another.
13. Our ________ who art in heaven. . . .
14. They that wait upon the Lord shall renew their ________
15. Though your ________ be as scarlet, they shall be as white as snow.
16. The valley of the ________ of death
17. The wages of sin is ________.
18. Whatsoever a man soweth, that shall he also ________.
19. Ye shall know the ________, and the ________ shall make you free.
20. Jesus said, "I am the Alpha and the ________."

Most Christians who tried the next two tests found them a challenge. Even literate Christians usually miss three or more.

Test 7: Geography

___	1. Mount Carmel	A. David hid from Saul here
___	2. Wittenberg	B. Hometown of Paul
___	3. Bethany	C. Transfiguration may have occurred here
___	4. Qumran	D. Paul preached a famous sermon here
___	5. Nicaea	E. "Ninety-five Theses" were posted here
___	6. Mars' Hill	F. Moses received the Ten Commandments here
___	7. En Gedi	G. Hagar took her son Ishmael here
___	8. Pool of Siloam	H. A Christian creed was written here
___	9. Antioch	I. The Triumphal Entry began here
___	10. Mount Sinai	J. The Dead Sea Scrolls were found here
___	11. Tarsus	K. Jesus appeared to two believers here after his resurrection
___	12. Mount Hermon	L. Mary and Martha lived here
___	13. Beersheba	M. Elijah defeated the prophets of Baal here
___	14. Emmaus	N. Blind man was healed here
___	15. Bethphage	O. Believers were first called Christians here

Test 8: Sayings that May Surprise You

1. We have __________ __________ those things which we ought to have done.
2. A good name is better than __________.
3. An outward and visible sign of an inward and spiritual __________.
4. Man proposes, God __________.
5. Giving honor unto the __________, as unto the weaker vessel
6. four __________ of the Apocalypse
7. Go to the __________, thou sluggard.

8. A ________ is not without honor except in his own country.
9. Put these words in the right order: Abandon, all, who enter here, ye, hope.
10. How ________ upon the mountains are the feet of them that bring good tidings.
11. The race is not always to the swift, nor the ________ to the strong.
12. Though he slay me, yet will I ________ [one or two words] him.
13. It is ________ ________ to give than to receive.
14. None doeth ________, no, not one.
15. The heavens are telling the ________ of God.
16. ________ your enemies . . . and do good to them . . . which despitefully use you.
17. Pride goes before ________.
18. ________ is the root of all evil.
19. Blessed are they that have not ________ and yet have believed.
20. Precious in the sight of the Lord is the ________ of his saints.
21. The ________ shall lie down with the ________.
22. He that spares the rod ________ ________ ________.
23. O Sacred Head, Now ________ (song)
24. How art thou fallen from heaven, O ________, son of the morning.
25. How lovely is thy ________, O Lord of Hosts.

For two thousand years, Christians have found the lists called for in Tests 9–14 important. We begin with the most central religious list of all time: a staple of your diet.

Test 9: Commandments

Name the Ten Commandments.

Test 10: Beatitudes

List the Beatitudes.

Test 11: Fruit of the Spirit

Name the nine-part "fruit of the Spirit" as listed by Paul.

Test 12: Seven Last Words

What were Christ's seven last "words" from the cross as recorded in the Bible? (They are actually seven statements.)

Test 13: Seven Deadly Sins

Name the seven deadly sins.

Test 14: Armor of God

When Paul said, "Put on the whole armor of God," what were the six items he named?

Tired of lists? Prefer to browse biographically? A word to the wise: Being familiar with Bible biographies won't help you with the next test—these are Christians who have made an impact on the world for their faith after the Book was complete. In a limited testing, three-fourths or more of the believers we asked chose the same wrong book as second to the Bible, and the same wrong preacher for the Great Awakening.

Test 15: Post-biblical Christians

__ 1. Who wrote *Confessions*? (A) Constantine (B) Augustine of Hippo (C) John Calvin (D) Pope John XXIII

__ 2. The monk who said, "Here I stand, I can do no other; God help me," and who began what is known as the Reformation was: (A) Ulrich Zwingli (B) Augustine of Hippo (C) Martin Luther (D) Charles Wesley

__ 3. The person who founded the Society of Friends, or Quakers, was: (A) Jonathan Edwards (B) William Penn (C) Mary Baker Eddy (D) George Fox

__ 4. "Make me an instrument of thy peace" is the: (A) Prayer of

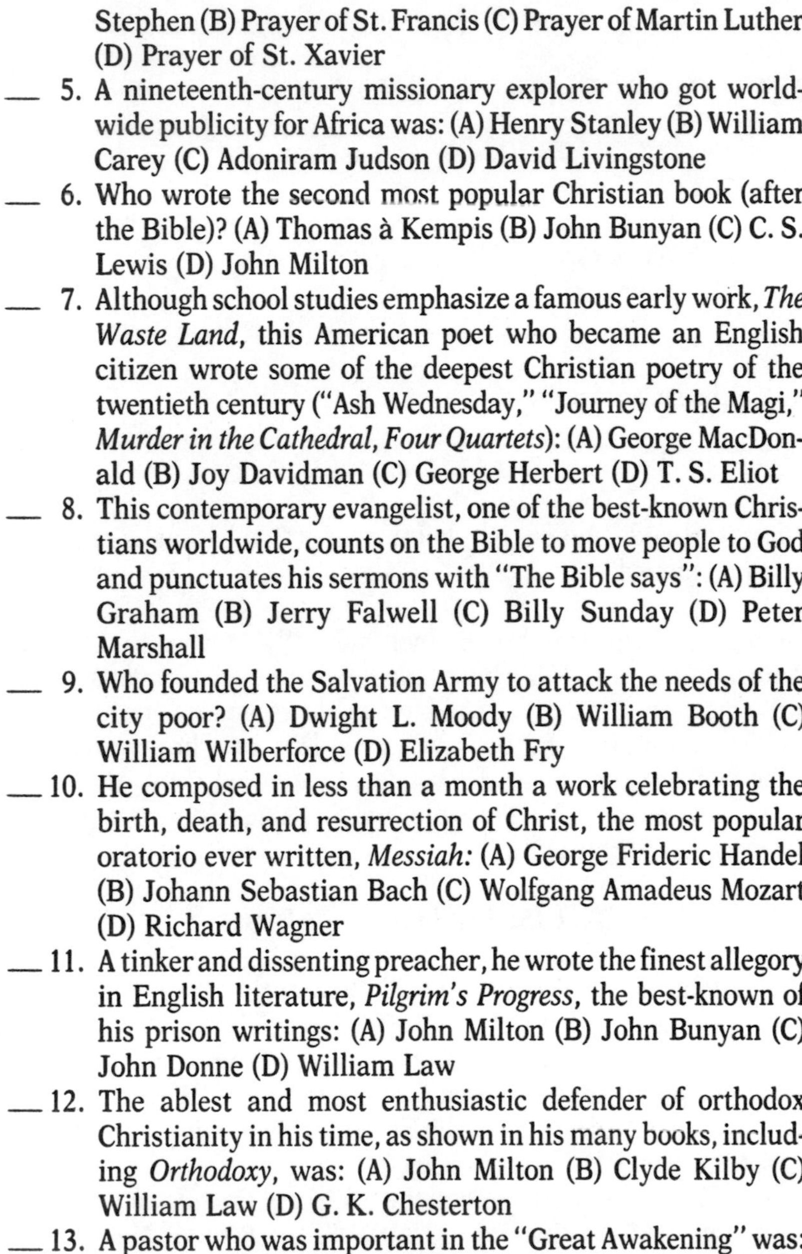

Stephen (B) Prayer of St. Francis (C) Prayer of Martin Luther (D) Prayer of St. Xavier

___ 5. A nineteenth-century missionary explorer who got worldwide publicity for Africa was: (A) Henry Stanley (B) William Carey (C) Adoniram Judson (D) David Livingstone

___ 6. Who wrote the second most popular Christian book (after the Bible)? (A) Thomas à Kempis (B) John Bunyan (C) C. S. Lewis (D) John Milton

___ 7. Although school studies emphasize a famous early work, *The Waste Land*, this American poet who became an English citizen wrote some of the deepest Christian poetry of the twentieth century ("Ash Wednesday," "Journey of the Magi," *Murder in the Cathedral, Four Quartets*): (A) George MacDonald (B) Joy Davidman (C) George Herbert (D) T. S. Eliot

___ 8. This contemporary evangelist, one of the best-known Christians worldwide, counts on the Bible to move people to God and punctuates his sermons with "The Bible says": (A) Billy Graham (B) Jerry Falwell (C) Billy Sunday (D) Peter Marshall

___ 9. Who founded the Salvation Army to attack the needs of the city poor? (A) Dwight L. Moody (B) William Booth (C) William Wilberforce (D) Elizabeth Fry

___ 10. He composed in less than a month a work celebrating the birth, death, and resurrection of Christ, the most popular oratorio ever written, *Messiah:* (A) George Frideric Handel (B) Johann Sebastian Bach (C) Wolfgang Amadeus Mozart (D) Richard Wagner

___ 11. A tinker and dissenting preacher, he wrote the finest allegory in English literature, *Pilgrim's Progress*, the best-known of his prison writings: (A) John Milton (B) John Bunyan (C) John Donne (D) William Law

___ 12. The ablest and most enthusiastic defender of orthodox Christianity in his time, as shown in his many books, including *Orthodoxy*, was: (A) John Milton (B) Clyde Kilby (C) William Law (D) G. K. Chesterton

___ 13. A pastor who was important in the "Great Awakening" was: (A) Henry Ward Beecher (B) Jonathan Edwards (C) Dwight L. Moody (D) Billy Sunday

___ 14. The best-known defender of the doctrine of the Trinity at the Council of Nicaea was: (A) Eusebius (B) Clement (C) Athanasius (D) Jerome

___ 15. A Bohemian priest and professor, he was burned at the stake for opposing the sale of indulgences and the veneration of images: (A) John Huss (B) John Knox (C) William Tyndale (D) Martin Luther

One of the best tests—and sometimes the hardest—of whether people know something is how easily they apply it. So our last test does that. Do you hear the Bible echoing everywhere in American culture? Politicians and preachers alike find it common fare. Martin Luther King, Jr., was one of those.

Test 16: Biblical Allusions in a Contemporary Speech ("I Have a Dream")

Find ten or more biblical allusions, phrases, or quotations in this excerpt from the best-known speech of Martin Luther King, Jr.:

Five score years ago, a great American, in whose symbolic shadow we stand today, signed the Emancipation Proclamation. . . . It came as the joyous daybreak to end the long night of [Negro] captivity. . . .

Now is the time to rise from the dark and desolate valley of segregation to the sunlit path of racial justice. Now is the time to lift our nation from the quicksands of racial injustice to the solid rock of brotherhood. Now is the time to make justice a reality for all of God's children.

. . . The whirlwinds of revolt will continue to shake the foundations of our nation until the bright day of justice emerges.

. . . Let us not seek to satisfy our thirst for freedom by drinking from the cup of bitterness and hatred.

. . . No, no, we are not satisfied and we will not be satisfied until justice rolls down like the waters and righteousness like a mighty stream.

I am not unmindful that some of you have come here out of great trials and tribulations. . . . Continue to work with the faith that unearned suffering is redemptive.

. . . I say to you today, my friends, even though we face the difficulties of today and tomorrow, I still have a dream. . . . I have a dream that one day this nation will rise up and live out the true meaning of its creed: "We hold these truths to be self-evident that all men are created equal."

. . . I have a dream that one day down in Alabama . . . little black boys and black girls will be able to join hands with little white boys and white girls as sisters and brothers.

. . . I have a dream that one day every valley shall be exalted, every hill and mountain shall be made low, the rough places will be made plain and the crooked places will be made straight, and the glory of the Lord shall be revealed, and all flesh shall see it together.

This is our hope. . . . With this faith we will be able to work together, to pray together, to struggle together, to go to jail together, to stand up for freedom together, knowing that we will be free one day.

This will be the day when all of God's children will be able to sing with new meaning: "My country 'tis of thee, / Sweet land of liberty, / Of thee I sing. . . ."

From every mountainside, let freedom ring. And when we allow freedom to ring, when we let it ring from every village, from every hamlet, from every state and every city, we will be able to speed up that day when all of God's children, black men and white men, Jews and Gentiles, Protestants and Catholics, will be able to join hands and sing in the words of the old Negro spiritual: "Free at last! free at last! thank God almighty, we are free at last!"

So how did you do? You may have found your lifetime diet wasn't varied or nourishing enough to prepare you for these tests. If so, the first thing on our reading list may be for you—read the Bible through, perhaps trying a three-year plan.

Or you may indeed have known more than you thought. If so, you are probably what we have been calling a literate Christian. Although you are a vanishing breed, you are not alone, as the next chapter explains.

Chapter 5

WHAT DO LITERATE CHRISTIANS KNOW?

In a cartoon, two children are walking along. Winthrop's friend says, "I found a strange word in this book I'm reading. It's 'apocryphal.' I wonder what it means."

Winthrop always has an answer: "That's easy. It's from the old nursery rhyme—'Sing a song of sixpence, apocryphal of rye.' "

His friend sighs: "I wish I knew all that hard stuff, like Winthrop does."[1]

One blue-collar worker, unlike the children in the cartoon, really does know "all that hard stuff"—he is well versed in the basics of the faith. He does not have a reputation as a great church leader but believes he is led of God to write. In no uncertain terms, he defends the faith and denounces the bad guys. He mentions, in passing, information that he and the ones he addresses have known all about from their youth upwards. He references the Old Testament freely. He even quotes the Jewish Apocrypha, although his audience does not consider it inspired. He cites a tradition he and his audience hold in common. But he is not writing in an intellectual journal to the middle-to-upper class; nor is he one who feels constrained to pedantically pass on the culture.

Jude and other obscurities

Is this anybody you know? It's not likely. He would be an anomaly in the American church.

But he would not be one in the New Testament church. The biblical Jude, a poor son of a carpenter, if tradition is correct, was not an aberration within the early church—he fit right in with Peter and John, the fishermen. Nevertheless, Jude's knowledge is impressive: within just a few lines he cited an apocryphal tradition about Michael; from the Old Testament he mentioned fallen angels, Judgment Day, Sodom and Gomorrah, hell, Cain, Balaam, Korah; and he passed on what the apostles said, as well as a description of the work of the three persons of the Trinity.

We don't know of many blue-collar types who are writing and leading in the church today. What this shows is how Christianity has changed; the brunt of the writing and the leading is done by the white-collar professional class. If a working-class person wants to lead, we often push him or her "up" to the other class. This is still another division among Christians—the difference in class between the ones who are contending publicly for the faith and the average Christian in the pew. Where are our literate Judes?

Jude, of course, has not been the only such person. Models from later times also challenge our ways. As an adolescent, Charles Spurgeon wanted "great things."[2] But as the son of an independent English preacher, Spurgeon was denied educational opportunities open to members of the establishment. He was nevertheless familiar enough with the scriptural phrasing that the Holy Spirit could bring Jeremiah 45:5 to his mind as a rebuke and a call to ministry: "Seekest thou great things for thyself?" Spurgeon went on to become *the* important preacher of his day, some say the greatest English preacher of the nineteenth century. Where are our literate teenage Spurgeons?

Even more striking was poet and abolitionist John Woolman, who, because he was from a poor family, could not go to school for as long as his richer and more cultured peers. But the Sundays that his family habitually spent in reading the Bible and good books meant he could read them for himself by the time he was seven; those habits set the direction for his life. He wrote a journal that is a classic for Christians.[3] Where are our literate young Woolmans? Where are the men and women from the working class serving as church leaders and writers now?

What the New Testament Jude knew and expected his audience to know is so unlike what literate Christians now know and expect their hearers to know. We are used to adapting to those gaps of age and education and class, not bridging them with better knowledge for everyone. But in order for young people of humble origins to rise to responsible leadership, we must make sure we pass on the core. Which should be our pattern—Jude or current practice?

Teraphim and the man on the street

Certain it is that Jude, Spurgeon, Woolman, and their counterparts contrast with one modern, well-educated, successful minister who speaks of biblical illiteracy and assures us that

> too many pastors talk a different language from the man in the street. The pastor's vocabulary is theological, academic and overly orthodox.
>
> One need only look at the average hymn language and understand how meaningless much of the theological language is. "Seraphim and Teraphim" are familiar words from an old, old hymn. But what in the name of seraphim do these words mean to unchurched people?
>
> Assuming that we successfully bring unchurched people into our Sunday morning services, will they understand what we are talking about? If they are biblically illiterate, will they understand the biblical terminology? And if they fail to understand, will they not turn off?[4]

In his outline, the writer, Robert Schuller, sees such "detachment from the world" as the second of "Eleven Attitudes That Hinder [Church] Growth." He does have a point about outreach to the unchurched. But, without knowing who the author was, three literate Christians we know took exception to some of what he is saying.

The first asked, "If *seraphim* goes now because the unchurched don't know it, when will *sin* and *reconcile* go because people don't know them?" Another wondered, "Whatever happened to positive 'detachment'—separation, as in Nehemiah 10?"

But the third laughed when she read it. " 'Seraphim and Teraphim' indeed!" she said. "Why didn't the editor catch that? The hymn 'Holy, Holy, Holy' doesn't have Rachel's household gods in it—it's '*cherubim* and seraphim.' "[5]

So who are literate Christians? Are these three typical? Besides *seraphim* and *teraphim*, what do contemporary Christians who are literate in the faith know? And what don't such Christians know? Finding that out is the start for recreating the consensus we have been calling for.

The knowledgeable Christian profiled

To answer such questions, we asked one hundred literate Christians we knew—of various ages, denominations, and geographical locations—to rank thousands of terms. Then the nationwide survey we described earlier was conducted, bringing a highly literate response, as we had hypothesized, from randomly selected *Christianity Today* subscribers. The resulting list tells us much of what literate Christians know. It is, like Hirsch's list, not exhaustive. Also like his, it is only tentative and preliminary in its details.[6] However, unlike his, the list we present can be seen as prescriptive, not merely descriptive. That is, we would contend that what literate Christians know is what every Christian needs to know.

We can profile who this knowledgeable Christian is. Judging from demographics from the *Christianity Today* survey, he (69 percent are men) is middle-aged and has attended graduate school, and most likely he has a graduate degree. He calls himself an "evangelical."[7]

He knows his Bible in and out—what others might call Bible trivia are intriguing to him. If presented with a picture of Roman armor, he could label it with the entire panoply of Paul's six-part armor of God (Eph. 6:13–17). Yet he does not know only trivia. To an encouraging degree, literate Christians also know and agree on what is important in the Bible.

The knowledgeable Christian has needed some years to become seasoned, so he may be older than the one who is not knowledgeable. The median age of those surveyed, forty-eight, puts them in the last generation that grew up poor but coping and strong during "the Depression" and "the War"—the last to grow up without childhood television, the last to grow up in a cultural consensus that with little dissent taught the values of education, hard work, family, and God.

Statistics show a qualitative difference between the childhood families of people who are culturally literate and those who are not; our informal demographics suggest that difference extends to the literate Christian. As a child, he was read to and became a reader, curious about the wider world that opened to him. Looking back, he has advantages of nurture that America is not likely to see again.

He knows much beyond the Bible: half the 1,031 terms on the survey list were understood by 95 percent or more of the subscribers responding.

The literate Christian also tends to know about denominations other than his own. The not-so-literate Christian does not. But even knowledgeable believers do not know as much cross-denominational terminology as a common language would require. And this lack of mutual knowledge contributes to the schism between high and low church. For instance, 49 percent of our surveyed *Christianity Today* subscribers were not sure what *lectionary* meant, and 69 percent were uncertain what *collect* meant.

Most important, the literate are more educated than those less literate. (A minority are self-educated. One older man, only a high-school graduate, reads the Jewish historian Josephus for fun.) They have much more schooling than the average Christian—an expensive priority. So again, it is partly a socioeconomic issue. Socioeconomics also contributes to the division between blue-collar and professional Christians that our reading of Jude calls into question and that the Book of James addresses. We ignore this to our peril.

A closer look at the literate Christian

A closer look here will describe the depth of knowledge possessed by the literate Christian.

Beyond Mother's Day

Days of feasting and fasting from the Christian calendar.

Somehow Mother's Day has become one of the most important days in the yearly cycle of church life. But the essence of the cycle of church celebrations and remembrances is grounded in the saving acts of God. Just as Jews celebrate a God-given cycle of feasts to commemorate the important events of their history (such as the Exodus from Egypt and the giving of the Law at Sinai), liturgical Christians celebrate the key events in the life of Jesus and the formation of the early church. Here are some of those days and seasons.

Advent. Four Sundays preceding Christmas. The church year begins every fall with a season of penitence and preparation. During this period, the church reads lessons from the Old Testament prophets anticipating the coming of Christ and reflects on how that period of waiting parallels our waiting for the Second Coming.

Christmas. December 25. A celebration of the Incarnation.

Holy Innocents. December 28. A remembrance of those who lost their lives when Herod the Great indiscriminately killed infants in an attempt to murder the Messiah.

Holy Name. January 1. Commemorating the day the infant Jesus would have been circumcised and formally named.

Epiphany. January 6. Celebrating the worship of the Magi.

The Baptism of Our Lord. The first Sunday after Epiphany. The Epiphany season extends to the beginning of Lent and focuses on the manifestations of Jesus' divinity, especially at his baptism and transfiguration.

Ash Wednesday. Forty days (excluding Sundays) before Easter. On Ash Wednesday, liturgical Christians enter into a season of penitence and preparation for Holy Week and Easter. The name comes from the ancient practice of applying ashes to the forehead to symbolize the truth of the reminder, "Remember that you are dust, and to dust you shall return."

Lent. From Ash Wednesday through Holy Week. The forty days are a reminder of the time Jesus fasted in the wilderness. The church meditates on Scripture lessons reminding believers of their sinfulness and their need of grace. In the worship of more liturgical denominations, the church forgoes such celebratory things as burning incense or using the word *Alleluia.*

Palm Sunday. One week before Easter. Also called the Sunday of the Passion. The liturgy for this first day of Holy Week begins by remembering Jesus' triumphant ride into Jerusalem. Many congregations celebrate by forming a procession and waving palm branches. However, the Scripture readings for this Sunday also focus on the crucifixion of Jesus, and the service ends on a somber note.

Maundy Thursday. Thursday in Holy Week. A remembrance of Jesus' last supper with his followers. In some churches the people wash one another's feet to recall Jesus' humility in serving the disciples.

Good Friday. Friday in Holy Week. Traditionally, churches held a long and somber service from noon until three as they meditated on Jesus' cross and passion. As contemporary living has made it less easy for people to attend such a service, services have shifted to the evening.

Easter. In the Western church, the Sunday after the full moon that occurs on or after the spring equinox on March 21. That is the short version of the definition. There are exceptions. Don't try to figure it out yourself. Check the calendar.

Easter is the celebration of Christ's resurrection from the dead. In recent years, many churches have been putting more emphasis on a service inherited from the early centuries of the church: the Easter Vigil, a service held during the night, featuring baptisms and confirmations.

Ascension Day. Forty days after Easter. During the Easter season the church meditates on the post-Resurrection appearances of Jesus. Then on Ascension Day it celebrates his enthronement in glory.

Pentecost. Fifty days after Easter. The birthday of the church, remembering the Holy Spirit's descent on the believers gathered in the Upper Room. Throughout the season following Pentecost, the Scripture lessons focus on the history of the early church in Acts.

Trinity Sunday. The Sunday after Pentecost. A celebration of the doctrine of the Trinity.

As we said, the paramount and most consistent (and therefore most unifying) thing the literate Christian knows is the Bible. He knows most of the Bible terms on the list; the survey indicated that the *average* respondent understood, not merely recognized, 88 percent of those mostly biblical terms. (He may be a little weaker than that in Bible geography.) Because he is an avid reader of many new versions of the Bible, using them for study, he is not always sure anymore how to quote a verse.

But he knows much Christian knowledge beyond the Bible, too.

Unsurprisingly, 97 percent of the respondents understood *excommunication, charismatic, celibacy, doctrine*. It may be a little more surprising that nonbiblical terms understood at the 85 percent level included *Apocrypha, canon, dogma, papacy, total depravity, A.D. 30, Eucharist, communion of saints, John Wesley*, and *John Calvin*. The literate Christian seems to be a bit weaker in church history than in most other areas; for example, fewer than half knew four of the eight dates listed. The terms least understood were extrabiblical. However, these are only relative weaknesses, as evidenced by the fact that at least half the respondents understood or recognized *all* the 1,031 terms surveyed.

The literate Christian may care passionately as well about some specialization of his—almost an avocation—that the average believer hasn't heard of or at least doesn't think much about. Maybe John Donne's *Holy Sonnets* speak to God for him. Or John Bunyan's pilgrimage to the Celestial City (or even Frodo's to Mount Doom) has become his own. Or he cries over John Milton or gets caught up in a Flannery O'Connor story. Or he is a Brahms or Bach buff. Or he immerses himself in Augustine or Tolstoy. Or he is healed in the soul by Rembrandt's paintings of Christ.

He may know the chronological details of Christian history; he feels the sweep of the Judeo-Christian heritage over thousands of years—and sees himself a part of that. He may give leisure time to Hebrew poetics or biblical archaeology, but even if he doesn't, he probably knows something about such things and cares enough about them that if that is your interest, he will talk with you.

Thus, the literate Christian reads widely. He may read a bit of C. S. Lewis almost every day—in fact, he may have been brought to Christ partly as a result of reading Lewis, as Prison Fellowship founder Charles Colson and U.S. Senator Mark Hatfield were.[8] He may know and love the poetry of George Herbert or Gerard Manley Hopkins, or contemporaries such as Luci Shaw; he may like to struggle along with not strictly Christian poets who want to know God on their own terms—perhaps Emily Dickinson or William Blake. However, he also reads—and, because he is a compulsive integrator, sees the spiritual implications—from and in—those who are not known as religious writers, such as Shakespeare or Dostoevski or Chaucer or Victor Hugo.

The knowledgeable Christian is aware of and sorry that most fellow believers are missing the cadence and nuances of the language of the King James Version (it probably was, in his childhood, "the one true version"). But he still appreciates and owns many other versions; he may have studied Greek or Hebrew and probably knows some of the difficulties in translating from them. In fact, he cares about the nuances of all language, feeling the weight of both sides of the argument in the feminist issue about using terms such as *man* and *mankind*.

The literate may be curious about the divergent Christian views on Creation; he may love to argue about how much Christians should involve themselves in politics, or which Greek text should be most trusted for the rendering of a particular New Testament passage, or how strong the Russian or Chinese churches really are. He may read and think about Kierkegaard or Barth, Bultmann or Bonhoeffer, story theology or form criticism or liberation theology.

Because knowing is so important to the literate Christian, he may, as in the seraphim incident, wish to set people straight. A nationally distributed newspaper article was headlined, "Could Kitty [Dukakis] and Barbara [Bush] Be Mary and Martha?"[9] It went on to identify "Marthas" as "delicate, deferent, and most of all devoted, the Weaker Vessels of popular proverb" and "Marys" as "independent and individualistic, interested in ideas and their application."[10] No knowledgeable Christian could forbear trying to straighten out the truths, half-truths, and errors that hopelessly confused Mary and Martha throughout the feature. The next week someone just had to write in:

> That editorial-page article . . . certainly shows the religious illiteracy of our day. . . .
>
> Actually, Martha was the sister who kept busy, and Mary was the one who sat at Jesus' feet. But none of your high-powered editorial help seemed to know that. . . .
>
> What scriptural lesson do we have in store for this Sunday? Will it be how Abel bumped off Cain? . . .[11]

But truth for the knowledgeable Christian is not just setting others straight. Because, for him, all truth is most powerfully God's truth—as it is for the makers of the list—he is linked with the past and with the arts. Malcolm Muggeridge speaks for him:

> [T]hroughout history, the words of the Gospel have inspired many of the noblest accomplishments of our civilization. . . . To the greater glory of these words Bach composed, El Greco painted, St. Augustine labored at his *The City of God* and Pascal at his *Pensées.*[12]

In fact, the literate man may see the same images and people marching down through time as Muggeridge does—he often treasures those same Christian artifacts of the past. He may even see himself in step with them, for he may have a stronger kinship with them than with some present-day Christians he knows. He may still make pilgrimages to view these places and these works.

Differences in knowledge

Being omnivorous readers, the one hundred knowledgeable Christians we surveyed in our first, more informal survey know the Bible and also much besides the Bible. But they are divided on how much of this knowledge—or even which particular terms and phrases—others should know or recognize. Should they promote the reading of Christian classics among people who are not even reading the Bible? Should people know all the varieties of Christian science that these Christians know, including such terms as *entropy* and *theistic evolution*? Do they have to be world Christians and know what is happening in the Soviet Union, South Africa, China? How much theology or philosophy do they need to know? Do all Christians need to know about current issues that have moral implications but aren't directly spiritual in nature, like *AIDS* or *euthanasia*?

The oldest group of the hundred who ranked terms by importance was interested in passing on theological words: *justification, sanctification,* and so on. The group in the middle age range was more issues oriented, apparently seeing these as relevant to all Christians (e.g., *abortion, apartheid,* and *polytheism* and other missions terms). But, in general, Christians of the hundred who ranked terms did not think it was important for believers to know anything that they did not view as central to the Christian faith, not even if those things were significant to them personally.

The initial survey confirmed that Christianity as it is perceived and practiced in America is determinedly relevant. Although they told us how they wrestled with the problem, when these hundred had to rank what was most or next-most important to Christian growth and consensus, there was no art, no literature. There was no history, not even church history or American history that comes from Christian roots, like the *Mayflower* and Plymouth Colony. They had little interest in terms not used by all denominations and little or no interest in other religions. There was high recognition of music (hymn titles, lines of songs), but low regard for its importance, even though for many of them music is observably influential in their daily walk. There were few philosophical or theological terms and few Greek or Latin terms. In general, the hundred who ranked terms did not see why Christians of the past or present should be called important unless they were preachers (no Jimmy Carter, no Robert E. Lee, for example). In sum, they did not think every believer needs to know (or even be aware of) Christian classics, theology, church history, denominational history, music, philosophy, the classical

© *LEADERSHIP*, 1983. Artist: Gerry Mooney. Concept: Jim Berkley.

languages, and contemporary Christians and Christian issues.

The loneliness of the literate Christian

Yet some of these very categories of Christian knowledge are the province of every literate Christian. Perhaps only his wife (or husband) knows about them, because with whom else can he or she share them? But they feed the literate Christian's soul and inform his life.

It is not hard to illustrate how this puts space between him and those others. The Christmas that this book was being written, one of the authors received a letter from a former student that referred to a poem many people don't know. She wrote, "The first time I met you . . . was also the first time I heard 'Journey of the Magi.' I don't believe I've ever been quite the same. Just this morning, I cried over it—yet again. We're having a few of the neighbors over tonight to celebrate the coming of the magi. None had ever heard the word 'epiphany.' [My husband] wants to read T. S. Eliot, but I feel it would be 'casting pearls before swine.' Not that the neighbors resemble swine in *any* way, but I just couldn't bear to have everyone ask, 'Yes, but what does it mean?' "

So the knowledgeable one is probably without a group to communicate with about these things that mean so much to him. In fact, depending on where he lives, there may be a chasm between him and the other Christians he is most often with. He may, therefore, be lonely.

And he may be your pastor. One of three respondents in the magazine survey was a member of the clergy. No doubt many others were in Christian service, perhaps as teachers. In that survey, the clergy understood 186 terms (18 percent of the terms) significantly better than laity. (Naturally, the terms showing the greatest difference between clergy and laity are theological.) This means that one-fifth of the pastor's tested Christian vocabulary is not shared by even most of the knowledgeable members of his church. No doubt he works at not talking above their heads, as he is admonished over and over by writers like Schuller. But that also means a good deal of his knowledge goes unshared. Thus, the clergy on one side and the laity on the other form just one more of the unbridged gaps in the American church that cause us to be such a fragmented body.

How do these gaps between the literate Christian and other Christians affect his attitudes? He may be seen as a know-it-all or show-off who puts other people down. (He probably doesn't intend that—it just naturally happens to him because of his curiosity and his heightened sense of the incongruous.)

That is why, even though he may be lonely, and even though he would love to open his heart to people about all this, he may not. Because he knows they don't usually know, and they don't sometimes care, perhaps he is unwilling to try, even though these things loom large in his Christian life. The more the life of the mind combined with the life of the spirit atrophies in our civilization, the stronger will be the longings of those like the literate Christian.

He is sensitive to his dilemma. He is only too aware that knowledge can "puff up" (1 Cor. 8:1). He holds in tension the paradox that the seeker of increased knowledge increases his own sorrow (Eccles. 1:18), but that the man is happy who finds wisdom and gets understanding (Prov. 3:13).

Not many wise are chosen, he knows, but he also takes comfort in knowing that some few were chosen who did special and significant work for God; three knowledgeable believers in the Bible were Moses, Daniel, and Paul. Outside of Christ himself, Moses and Paul were the outstanding men of their Testaments. All three were at home in two cultures, their own and the dominating one of the day. In preparing them, God took care to give them the best educations their world systems afforded.

With all his knowledge, and yet with his uncertainty about sharing it, no wonder this Christian asks, "How much of what I know do others need to know?" Such knowledgeable ones can weep over the ignorance of other believers. And sometimes they can boil over at the lack of study because they believe that faithful does not equate with literate but does *relate* to literate. They are not always middle-agers looking back, either; a Christian college freshman said of her fellow students, "You just want to open up their heads and pour all this knowledge in that they need. It's hard when you see them not doing what they set out to do. You get angry."

We have seen that literate Christians know the Bible and hold much else in common. But they are widely diverse (perhaps even divided) on what others should know. They know "all that hard stuff" and would love to be surrounded by present-day Judes. They would love for every brother and sister of every race, class, age, denomination, and education to know and live by a higher level of Christian knowledge. And they would love to pass on what they have found so central in their lives to the newer generation of Christians.

Chapter 6

HAS THE TORCH BEEN PASSED OR DROPPED?

Scene: A public university classroom in the Bible Belt.

Assignment: Read "The Sermon on the Mount" from a freshman rhetoric textbook.

Responses: Agnosticism—" '[y]ou shouldn't believe everything you read' . . . applies in this case." Dismissal—"A . . . fallback is that certain beattitudes [*sic*] are irrelevant to current life-styles." Anger—"This is a direct quote from the Bible. Why is it in the Literature Book? . . . I see no point in this. College is a time to reassess your life." The angriest response—"The things asked in this sermon are absurd. To look at a woman is adultery. That is the most extreme, stupid, inhuman statement that I have ever heard."

Analysis by the teacher: "Was this all that remained of the old-fashioned piety I had expected? . . . [T]he Bible remains offensive to honest, ignorant ears, just as it was in the first century."[1]

Does this scene show that "In God We Trust" is still true? Is it the motto of Americans, especially the younger generation? Certainly most of our youth, ages fourteen to twenty-five, know firsthand about sex, drugs, alcohol, and divorce. But what these young Americans don't know and don't care about, David Gates writes in *Newsweek*, is "scary":

> Homegrown Jeremiahs have often likened the United States to the Roman Empire in decline. But in one respect, the analogy no longer holds. The Visigoths are not at the gates: they're in the next room watching TV. They're America's own young, and most of them don't know from Visigoths—or Jeremiah. . . .
>
> Young Americans aren't so hot on more "relevant" history, either. One recent study of 1,000 16- to 18-year-olds found that over a quarter of them thought Franklin D. Roosevelt was president during the Vietnam War. . . . Two-thirds can't date the Civil War within 50 years. . . . And one-third think Columbus sailed for the New World sometime after 1750.[2]

Young people today know Genesis as the name of a rock band or a planetary project in a *Star Trek* film, but not as the first book of the Bible. They know Pepsi and the new generation, but not heaven and the everlasting generation; "L.A. Law," but not God's law. They know who makes *280 Z*'s, but not the Alpha and Omega who made them. They know Nikes and the winning team, but not victory in Jesus. They know how to look at "Days of Our Lives," but not how to look into the days of their lives.

Gates is pessimistic, concluding that unless young people are somehow made less apathetic, "civilization may perish simply because nobody bothered to pass it on."[3]

Is it as bad as he says? (After all, the explanation could be that older Americans know more than younger ones because knowledge naturally increases with age.)

Yes, we answer, it is bad—it may even be fatal. Our observation of young people of the same age over a thirty-year period tells us that.

Are young Christians literate?

But what about the *Christians* of this younger generation? What do they know? And what don't they know? Has the torch been passed to them, or has it been dropped?

One way to find out what they know is to ask them. So we did.

Perhaps partly because they have had less time to learn, we found no highly literate Christians in the pretwenty group of our one hundred selected Christians. The average eighteen-year-old Christian responding to a national *Campus Life* survey is also markedly less literate in the Christian faith than her middle-aged counterpart.[4] *Only 2 percent of the 1,031 terms were understood by 95 percent of the subscribers responding.* That contrasts with 50 percent of the terms being understood by 95 percent or more of the *Christianity Today* subscribers responding. This is no ho-hum, garden-variety, business-as-usual knowledge gap.

The good news is that the young respondent knows what we all consider the heart of the core—such terms and phrases as *Christ* and *Jesus Christ, "Do unto others as you would have them do unto you," the Ten Commandments, "Love your enemies," "God so loved the world that he gave his only begotten son," hell,* and *the Crucifixion* were understood by 96 percent or more of the respondents. The bad news is that of the 1,031 terms and phrases tested, only 120 were known above the 90 percent level; it would be hard to carry on a meaty conversation with other Christians with a 120-term or even a 120-phrase vocabulary.

Fewer than half knew such biblical injunctions and phrases as *"to obey is better than sacrifice," "grace to help in time of need," "The heavens declare the glory of God,"* and *"Search the Scriptures; for in them ye think ye have eternal life."* Only four out of ten knew *"Except a corn of wheat fall into the ground and die, it abideth alone"* and *"The heart is deceitful above all things and desperately wicked."*

A nationwide Gallup poll resulted in similar findings. One-fourth of the surveyed youth who are regular churchgoers could not name any of the Ten Commandments, and only two-thirds could name three (*don't steal, don't commit adultery, don't murder*). (Happily, churched teenagers exceeded the unchurched by an average of 14 percent on whether they were able to name specific commandments.)[5]

Two typical incidents illustrate the statistics. A public high-school teacher in Florida got a Christmas card with a message written on it, "Thy word is a lamp unto my feet, and a light unto my path." The student had carefully credited this as a song by Amy Grant and Michael W. Smith. "Thank you," the teacher said. "I hope you know this is from the Bible, too." The student was surprised. "Oh, really? I didn't know that." In another state, two-thirds of Christian college juniors in a literature class did not know that *The Scarlet Letter* is an *A* and that it stands for *adultery*, although the subject of the book and its study of the effects of sin are relevant to the lives of their generation.

So the national survey under the aegis of *Christianity Today* magazine has confirmed about Christian young people what was already shown by local surveys, observation, and parallel studies such as those currently receiving wide media coverage: They, too, do not know what they need to know. How will they be able to lead the church if they don't know what the church is all about?

Causes of Christian illiteracy

Why don't these young people who name the name of Christ know what they need to know? Bluntly and more broadly: Why don't they want to know? We have some tentative answers for who they are and how they got that way.

An obsession with their age group alone. Several cultural analysts have complained of the widespread narcissism (not only among the young) in our society. One contributor to the narcissism of young people, Christians included, is that all too often they are members of *their* generation—period. They are predisposed to feel no connection with the church as a community across the generations. Susan Littwin, author of *The Postponed Generation*, writes of young adults, "These are special children, brought up to be individuals. . . . They never felt they had a role to play in the community or the family, and certainly never believed that they might have to sacrifice their individuality."[6]

The narcissism of Christian young people has been fortified because they, like others their age, don't join the larger culture until they are eighteen to twenty-two years olds, or even older; therefore, they have no commitment to it. The problem is accentuated in the church because, as Christian educator Mark Wade says, our congregations are age segmented: "We'll have to decide if we want that kind of efficiency—or if we want community."[7]

Insecurity about the future. Narcissism is a convoluted syndrome that may be the main reason young people don't know what they need to know. In other words, their generation does not care about anything but *me* and *now*, as educator Howard Macy, among many others, observes. And what is behind that? Macy names two "destructive elements . . . uncertainty about the future and uncertainty about one's own identity and importance."[8]

A youth pastor we know agrees: "With the technology [of nuclear weaponry]—after all, we can be blown up any time—[young] people can't comprehend life and don't feel they're in control. So they're not trying to change. They say, 'That's the way it is.' The young have so many pressures at such an early age. They don't know that the fear of the Lord can be a power for them." He explained that the fear of the Lord could be the opposing and more powerful fear that would release them from the fear of an uncertain future.

Ultraindividualism. Narcissism is constantly being reinforced by America's ultraindividualism. The Japanese, for example, find our every-man-for-himself work model incomprehensible. What happens in the workplace is even more pervasive after work. Americans rejoice in the liberty and freedom so envied by non-Americans, but they see liberty and freedom simply as individualism. Paradoxically, the teens who are so much alike also clamor for rugged individualism. They often cannot name parts of the Bill of Rights, but they know it means "I've got my rights."

Experience satiation. An additional facet of this rampant self-absorption is that the culture is experience satiated, and the Christian sector is not immune. One prominent Roman Catholic educator tells us that if our education in Christian and parochial schools and in Sunday school isn't working—if it does not meet the experience-based objectives he recommends—we should change our style of educating or drop the education.[9] An educator friend of ours says another instance is that the majority of current Christian music—

"feel good" music—is experience based just like the world's. Yet another example is that holy living is "out." The emphasis instead is on the filling of the Holy Spirit as an experience that feels good, not as an enablement for the dailiness of life and the consistency and discipline that are implied by the fruit of the Spirit.

The whole "experience" movement is contrary to the biblical thrust, a negative trend almost certain to trap pubescent young people. But we think the best way to address it is simply to call for balance: We need to educate the whole person. This does not exclude experience, for humans do share a body with the animal world.

How Times Change
Some bad words that used to be good.

cult. From the Latin word for "worship," the word *cult* entered the English language about 1650, and for centuries after, it simply meant the homage, worship, or devotion paid to God, a saint, or an important person (such as when *The Oxford English Dictionary* lists a reference to "the cult of Wordsworth"). Some time in the twentieth century the word came to have a pejorative connotation: "a religion or sect considered to be false, unorthodox, or extremist" (*Random House Dictionary of the English Language)*. Scholars still use the word as a neutral term for a system of worship. But *cult* has such a bad reputation that publishers have been sued for using it to describe an out-of-the-mainstream religious group.

pious. What Christian wouldn't want to be known as "careful of the duties owed by created beings to God"? That is how Dr. Johnson defined *pious*. But call most Christians "pious" and they shudder. Like *bad* in black English, *pious* has come to mean its opposite, layered with overtones of hypocrisy and the false façade.

priest. It started life as the Greek *presbuteros,* then graduated to become the Latin *presbyter* and then *prester.* These words meant "elder," referring to an older person as well as to a church office. (For example, Paul told Titus to "ordain elders in every city" [Titus 1:5]). As early as A.D. 375, the word entered the English language as *préost,* referring only to Christian clergy. English borrowed from Latin a different word *(sacerd)* to refer to pagan and Jewish priests. Since the Reformation most Protestants would rather suck sour lemons than call their clergy "priests." (After all, in the high Middle Ages, priestcraft seems to have hit an all-time low.) Instead, they prefer to have "elders"—a translation of *presbuteros,* which is where it all started.

However, our culture now is not emphasizing looking *at* as well as looking *along* an experience—both analyzing and experiencing.[10]

Apathy. The knot of narcissism is pulled still tighter because most of the young generation don't believe in anything or passionately care about anything. (In a no-doubt apocryphal story, a student was asked, "What is the difference between ignorance and apathy?" His answer: "I don't know and I don't care.") And since these Christian youth are like their peers in this regard as in many others, they have caught the culture's apathy. The one absolute Allan Bloom says students come to college with is that there are no absolutes. They are saying, "Your 'truth' is as good as my 'truth.'" They are very tolerant of beliefs because their own beliefs are so tenuous. If all truth is relative, why care about it? So nothing is worth passionate involvement. Bloom sees this relativism as a major cause of the closing of the American mind.[11]

The destructive messages of rock music. Bloom does believe young people are passionate about one thing: rock-and-roll music. His indictment of that music could have been written by an evangelical:

> [T]his generation . . . [has an] addiction to music. . . . It is their passion; nothing else excites them. . . . When they are in school and with their families, they are longing to plug themselves back into their music. Nothing surrounding them—school, family, church—has anything to do with their musical world. . . . Young people know that rock has the beat of sexual intercourse. . . . The words implicitly and explicitly describe bodily acts that satisfy sexual desire and treat them as its only natural and routine culmination for children who do not yet have the slightest imagination of love, marriage or family. This has a more powerful effect than does pornography on youngsters.[12]

Bloom believes that rock music prevents learning, blocks community (even with teenage peers), and hinders learning the values of the family; that it divides the generations when it invades the family; and that it degrades youths' values when it pervades their lives. A youth pastor asked his Christian high schoolers about non-Christian rock, "Why do you listen to things you don't believe in?" Their answer: "It's okay to listen to it because I don't believe it and so it won't hurt me." They had the same attitude toward watching music videos and R-rated movies. But their pastor knows better; he knows how these things affect him, even though he's more mature than they are.

The opiate—passivity. Television, rock and roll, and the easy life have made our youth passive. Information overload has made them passive: There is just too much to learn. When it comes to learning, young people want to be entertained or they will tune it out, just as they switch TV channels. Everything must be fun. Youth workers tell us that it's hard to bring them into church because not everything in church is fun; that because the youth are just let go and are not taught any responsibilities, it is an uphill battle to involve them; and that they need to know it takes effort to be a Christian. They don't realize that, and they don't realize that everyone—old or young—must take the first step.

Our cultural indifference to reading. Young people are not readers. This is not surprising, since their parents rarely prize reading. At one Christian college, a fifth of the students said their parents had never read to them. The lack of reading is partly the result of the strong vocational orientation of Americans: Parents don't read because it doesn't seem practical. They are more concerned with "Can my kid operate computers and get a job?" It fits the American obsession with the bottom line. These parents have never learned for the sake of learning, so neither have their children. In this way the value of education has become attenuated and relativized by the marketplace.

So it follows that young people who read little of anything do not read their Bibles. One researcher found out that "in the liveliest evangelical churches, people strongly feel they should read the Bible daily, but only around 15 percent do so." By the way, they do not doubt that God has the authority to tell them what to do: "The people we surveyed had no qualms about the authority of the Bible," *The Student Bible* coeditor Tim Stafford explains. "Youth especially had an almost magical view of the book. They believed that it offered

Proverbial People

Old Testament characters in everyday English.

Just as Charles Dickens's Ebenezer Scrooge became a symbol of stinginess, so certain Old Testament characters have a permanent place in our conversation as embodiments of certain vices and virtues.

Jehu. To say someone "drives like Jehu" is to say he drives fast and furiously. The reference is to a general who led a bloody coup d'état against the weak King Ahab and his wicked queen Jezebel (see below). In 2 Kings 9, a watchman in the city of Jezreel sees an approaching group of riders. He announces to young King Jehoram, son of Jezebel, "The driving is like the driving of Jehu . . . for he driveth furiously."

Jezebel. To call a woman a "Jezebel" is to call her an evil influence. The biblical Jezebel was married to Ahab, king of Israel. She was not, however, an Israelite, and she promoted the worship of Baal and Asherah, the deities of pagan fertility worship. She was also responsible for the murder of many of the prophets of Yahweh. Her name is associated with ruthlessness, for she had Naboth stoned to death in order to gain his vineyard for her husband. Jezebel's name is also associated with the false allure of painted beauty. In the final scene of her life, she primped and preened before meeting the victorious Jehu who had slain her son in battle. The unimpressed general had her thrown from her upper window to her death.

Job. The "patience of Job" is proverbial. Shakespeare even made Job into a symbol: "I am as poor as Job, my Lord, but not so patient" *(Henry IV, Pt. II, I, ii)*. After losing his property and children to robbers and natural disasters, Job worshiped, and said, "Naked came I from my mother's womb, and naked shall I return; the LORD gave and the LORD has taken away; blessed be the name of the LORD." The author of the Book of Job adds, "In all this Job did not sin or charge God with wrong." Later in this long narrative poem, Job does level charges of unfairness against God, but it is Job's patience under duress and not his protests of innocence that have earned him a place in our language.

Job's comforters. Also from the Book of Job come these false friends. A "Job's comforter" is one who means to sympathize with you in your trouble, but makes you feel worse by reminding you that your trouble is all of your own doing. Job's friends were just that helpful.

the words of life. There was only one sticking point: They did not read the Bible. When they tried, they could rarely understand it."[13]

Adults, we should also point out, are affected by many of the same pressures as the youth. If they watch television, listen to pop radio, and go to popular movies, they will imbibe these same values that are targeted at teens. The result is that many younger adults in their twenties and thirties are, like their younger counterparts, to some extent dulled in their ability to read and understand the Bible.

Why the torch has been dropped

After a survey of these obstacles to a literate youth culture, we are back to our opening question: Have we dropped the torch before we could get it into their hands? After all, Paul made transferring the essentials of the faith the responsibility of those who gave it: "Pass on . . . these teachings," he wrote to Timothy (1 Tim. 4:11, NEB). What has interfered with the passing process? Some of us are not enough different from the younger generation to be faithful proclaimers. If so, do they see us as offering them a blazing torch, or just a flickering candle?

But the persistence of pockets of young people who do know what they should shows the torch can be passed and has been passed to some. We will want to find those pockets and discover how to duplicate the work of those who have guided their learning. (And it is work.) Why do some know and some not know? What has been taught in the church, school, and family?

What churches teach

In one two-year confirmation class, a teacher told her students that they would not be learning "just Bible facts" because there was not enough time to do so. "More importantly, we must deal with what portion of religion is truly relevant to your daily lives." In the light of that, she said they must study loving one's neighbor, social action, personality conflicts, alcohol and drugs, as well as how their denomination governs itself and its historical background. She explained that these other facts, from the Bible, were dealt with in Sunday school. The immediate implication of this is to deny the relevance of memorizing verses and learning the books of the Bible, but the wider implication is to deny the relevance of the Bible to the daily lives of young people. Something is wrong with confirmation nationwide: Nearly half (45 percent) of those now unchurched have received confirmation training.[14]

What does the church teach in the youth group? Many times the group can be cohesive for fellowship, but weak on learning because of the overweening yen for relevance. The youth group does have more impact than Sunday school. Why has that happened? One group of first-year Bible college women was critical of what they had learned in Sunday school. They said they had been taught the same Bible stories over and over—David and Goliath, Jonah and the whale, and so on. And one respondent pointed out that even the stories they knew were different from the way they really are in the Bible (she mentioned that nobody had ever said Job had *four* friends).

Another thing the church has taught them, as we have already charged, is the primacy of relevance. As one young woman told us, "I feel like I am *only* nineteen. I have spent the last seven years going through adolescence. . . . My concerns have basically been getting to know myself and growing up—and I feel that I haven't had the priority of becoming biblically intelligent." How different that is from the Jewish boy who became an adult on the occasion of his *bar mitzvah* at age twelve, and from Jesus, who at twelve was talking with the teachers at the temple and telling his earthly parents that he must be about his "Father's business" (Luke 2:49).

In this exaggerated desire for relevance, the legitimate cart has edged up in front of the horse. Surely we shouldn't ignore biblical doctrines just because they are not popular. For instance, the church has softened its teaching because it doesn't like hellfire and brimstone preaching. We are not giving a clear message of heaven and hell. Jesus talked far more about hell than we do. Surely we should not center on adolescent self-esteem when the Bible doesn't. Such examples show that we have gotten it backward: Surely we shouldn't teach looking to the Bible to prooftext our concerns rather than looking to the Bible to find out God's concerns.

Young people have learned in our churches that salvation is central. But as a result, they believe salvation is enough. "Just skip the details," they seem to be saying. The day of "easy believism" is not past. This is a problem common to evangelicals that is based upon a distorted understanding of the great Reformation truth that we are saved "by grace . . . through faith, and . . . not of works." Much of the church has nearly excluded the other side of that truth, even though Paul stresses it in the next verse: we are "created . . . for good works . . . that we should walk in them" (see Eph. 2:8–10, NKJV). That atmosphere in the church has created the theological lens youth are reading through; unintentionally, it has taught them to think that they can go on sinning because God will endlessly indulge them.

The family and education

Probably the main answer to the question of why young people are religiously illiterate is that they have been deprived by their elders of some essentials, such as those in Deuteronomy—learning how to incorporate God's principles into everything they do from the time

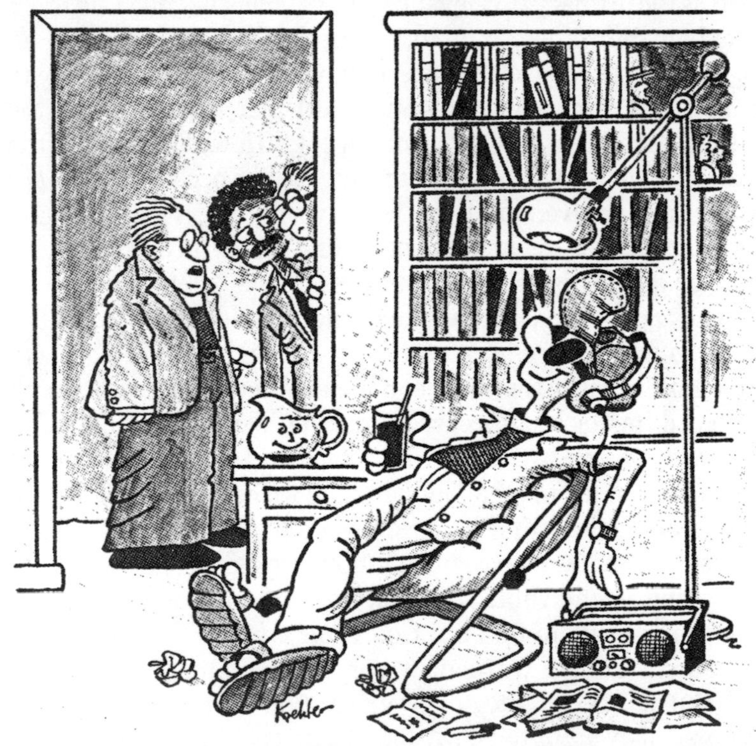

"Him? He's my assistant pastor. I believe he is in the process of relating the gospel to the nineties."

they get up in the morning until they go to bed at night (6:7–9). They have been deprived of the time and love and care—physical and spiritual and emotional—that they should have had. That is primarily a family problem. Part of what has been lost in the family is the model father, both loving and authoritative. This powerfully affected the way these youth as children knew God and whether they now want to know more. Many have gotten a permissive kind of love instead of the kind a father must show in order to demonstrate how the heavenly Father loves. As James Dobson writes, "It is a well-known fact that a child identifies his parents with God, whether or not the adults want that role. . . . To show our little ones love without authority is [a] . . . serious . . . distortion of God's nature."[15]

But because many of these young people were let go to do their own thing, they gained no concept of the obedience that is requisite to building in the heavenly Father's authority. Now they find it hard to obey God's injunctions, such as reading his Word, living a holy life, learning more about him. Their lack of discipline makes it hard to be disciples; their lack of discipline equates with lack of ability to carry things through even when they want to.

How impoverished these mostly "rich" youngsters are! They have everything except what they really need. They have been given only big-ticket items and not the day-to-day, hands-on intangibles "without money and without price" that they need to thrive (Isa. 55:1). This has gone to such an extreme that perhaps never since Christianity began, when Jesus talked about the Laodicean church, has a generation been so rich and yet so poor. And, like the Laodiceans, they don't really know how poor they are (Rev. 3:17).

What the schools teach

If churches and families are not teaching Christian youth what they need to know, should we count on the schools? But it was the school who taught youth that everything must be relevant to their lives. So much of the traditional curriculum has been dropped, little by little for the past fifty years, as being irrelevant—a trend that has escalated since the watershed of the sixties. So a young person's attitude toward anything not perceived as immediately applicable to him or her personally is, "Forget it." Their not knowing the historical facts we have cited is a symptom of their attitude toward "irrelevant" history in general. That is reflected in the current phrase for leaving—an alternative for "I'm outta here": "I'm history." How relevant can the history of the Israelites seem to these teens who do not know much about Columbus, Roosevelt, or the Vietnam War?

School and the mass media have also taught them that God is not part of this culture—he rarely makes an appearance in a school or a textbook. Paul C. Vitz's 1985 study, funded by the federal government, asked:

> Are public school textbooks biased? Are they censored? The answer to both is yes. And the nature of the bias is clear: Religion [and] traditional family values . . . have been reliably excluded from children's textbooks. . . . [N]ot one word or image in any book [of the 60 social studies texts studied] shows any form of contemporary representative Protestantism.[16]

But it goes beyond the "neutral" absence of religion from the classroom. "I believed in God," a college freshman wrote, "until my high school English teacher helped me become smarter." His college professor adds, "The irony was that, according to the same essay, his parents (whose taxes paid his teacher) had tried to raise him as a believing church-goer."[17]

Such an approach ignores the profound influence of the Judeo-Christian heritage on the nation. It ignores the whole "Year of the Evangelical" that *Newsweek* announced in 1976, and the dominant role Christ and his church play in the lives of millions of Americans. (In 1976 one-third said they had been born again, and in 1988 two-thirds said they had made a commitment to Christ.)[18]

How can our youth be helped?

So in the face of all this, we ask ourselves: What can we do to help young people grow to be faithful and literate Christians? Fortunately, help for this generation is on the way. Some more positive trends may ease their stresses and especially smooth the road for their younger siblings. Something is happening—in the church, the family, the school, and to some extent in the society at large: The alarm bells are ringing out there. This is a society that clearly and loudly and widely publicizes criticism of the deadening philosophies we have reported, like materialism, ultraindividualism, narcissism, relativism, pragmatism, anti-intellectualism, vocationalism. Such diagnostic publicity is healthy, for diagnosis precedes cure. Many see we're in a car without a steering wheel that is on a collision course. But Americans are activists; once told what needs to be done, they try to do it, and often succeed in avoiding collision that seems inevitable.

The best thing we can do is help our young people take control of their own destiny. The Bible makes everyone accountable for his or her own choices. So they need to look to themselves to see the problem: Are they really faithful to do what they know to do?

In this broken generation in a broken world, they will have to decide, "Do I want to be made whole?" That is the first step. God is in the business of making people whole, over a period of time, if they will take that first step. The J. B. Phillips version of 2 Corinthians 5:17 reflects the truth that this change is both instantaneous and gradual: "When someone becomes a Christian he *becomes* a brand new person inside. He is not the same any more. A new life *has begun!*" (emphasis ours).

These young people claim to know Christ—but that's all. If they can once decide to take the step—if they once decide that they want to be made whole and that they won't settle for anything less, even if it will be painful—they will want to break from the pack. They will then see the need for a radical shift in lifestyle, away from the thing-oriented society, from the antiknowledge trend, from immediate pleasure, from the "me first" syndrome. Some past generations of Christians could go along with the American society, could "go with the flow," because it was flowing out of a Christian consensus. This is the very thing no Christian, young or old, can do now that the Christian consensus is gone.

So these young people are faced with two alternatives as old as the human race. They can do nothing, and become more and more narcissistic until they pine away, like Narcissus in classical mythology. That is to say, "The man who loves himself is lost," as Jesus warns (John 12:25, NEB). Or they can decide to take action against their self-centeredness by cutting through the knot of narcissism.

This, then, is the second thing we can do to help our youth. We can help them have the courage to be different, like Daniel. His generation and society, even more than ours, was being culturally fractured, annihilated. But despite his youth he believed he had to stand up to the social system of his enemies, the very people who had total power over his earthly fate. There were no guarantees he would succeed. There were no promises others would join him. But he stepped out. His attitude to the pagan authority was respectful dissent. They told him he had to learn the enemy language and literature; to this young Jewish man nothing could have seemed more irrelevant (and perhaps evil). How could he know that God was preparing him through that very learning for the high positions in the enemy government that would be his life's work? But he accepted their teaching.

And God honored his obedience. Did Daniel think he would have to stand alone, that he might fail? No matter—he did move out from the crowd. It turned out that others joined him, others who would later stand up for God even though it meant the fiery furnace. Our young people, too, can go it alone, but even if they have to stand by themselves where they are, even if others do not join them, they will not really be alone, for they are with believers, living and dead, from every generation, and they have the promise of the One who will never leave them.

Although her circumstances are modern, one young woman overcame, as Daniel did, obstacles no teen should face: illegitimacy; her father's alcoholism; parents who beat her, didn't love her, and were not religious; and her own religious liberalism. Her conversion when she was in college was strengthened by the Navigators' "B-rations" (basic memory verses), by Bible study ("I read the Bible and every word leaped off the page"), and by her discipler. She is Roberta Hestenes, known for her commitment to biblical teaching and chosen in 1987 as the first woman president of a college in the evangelical Christian College Coalition.[19]

A high-school girl, one among many, in her own way is also doing what Daniel did. "But at first I was kind of scared," the girl we'll call Julie said, " 'cause I felt that if I would go and do this that I would lose my friends' friendship. . . . But then finally I just realized that God was more important." So she stepped out to become a Christian, and her friends saw the difference. After one of them watched her life for two months, he testified, "Last Sunday night I accepted the Lord. The main reason I did this is because [of] the change in Julie." The chain reaction included one of his friends: He, too, was converted to Christ that Sunday night.

Another young Daniel is very much a part of this generation. He likes a messy room, one earring, and rock music (although his is Scripture based). But as a junior in college he takes high schoolers he is befriending to his home and to where they will get the gospel in concerts. Knowledgeable and caring, last summer he was teaching a high-school group about holy living, using Jerry Bridges's *Pursuit of Holiness*.[20]

Some entire groups are Daniels. For twenty years a group of fifty to one hundred Illinois high-school young people have committed themselves to a choir. They give up every Wednesday evening and sing for at least forty Sunday morning services during the school year. Through presenting anthems and musicals, they have memorized such biblical texts as the Beatitudes, the life and words of the apostle Paul, and many narratives from Genesis to Revelation. They have been singled out as youth who are different from most of their peers because of their commitment to Christ. They have been written about in their school and city newspapers and have appeared and been interviewed on television and radio. They have witnessed their faith to others, even though it means being different and sometimes being ridiculed. But they have stuck with it—because they have a cohesive group that has stuck with them. Parents, brothers, sisters, and friends have come to Christ through the music and testimony of these young people.[21]

Can the torch be picked up?

The jury remains out, sorting through all this evidence. Can most young Christians really say "In God We Trust"? They don't know much of what they need to know because, in general, they are far too like the rest of their generation—narcissistic in their inconsistency, ultraindividualism, experience satiation, and relativistic apathy. Their narcissism connects them to the rock music and media of this world, but disconnects them from commitment, motivation, family, and reading. Most don't know much of what they need to know because the family, the church, the school, and the society—despite some heroic efforts and some isolated successes—have not been able to break through that narcissism to teach them.

Yes, the torch has been dropped. Many Christian youth do not know what they should. But here and there young people, like modern Daniels, are picking up the torch again, and running with it. May their tribe increase.

Chapter 7

WHAT MUST WE DO?

Judy is a young mother upset about the state of families in America. She believes the Lord has called her to stay home with her children—even though that often means doing without things she would like them to have. "The family is my job," she says. And as part of that job, she plans to fight, within her own sphere of influence, to restore Christian knowledge in the family and in the church.

Of course, all Christian parents, whether or not they work outside the home, have a responsibility for training their own young people and the youth of the church. But Judy, and others like her who have made a sacrificial commitment to devoting the major portion of their time and energy to family and church, have a special opportunity. What should they do to make the most of it?

We believe that teaching young people things such as Bible stories, hymns, and the stories of great Christians can do much to build Judy's family—and to rebuild the family as an institution.

But one warning must precede any discussion of strategies: *Education is not a sure cure.* The *New Oxford Review* says, "There are worse things than ignorance. . . . [O]ne discerns among the educational reformers the hoary American conviction that more and better education will heal many of our ailments . . . [if we] inject enough culture and learning into the nation's bloodstream. . . . To believe that, is to be truly ignorant."[1] The cultural problems that have helped to erode Christian knowledge cannot be solved merely by education. It is seductive to think education could solve all our problems—but there is no quick fix. We are in for a long and dirty war, not a swiftly settled border skirmish.

Seeing education as a cure-all can also lead to the "facts only" fallacy: that all we need to do is communicate certain terms and propositions. We need the facts of our faith, of course, but also the sights, sounds, and smells (for example, the images and the music), the experiencing and understanding of our faith—a balanced and full knowledge. The way to keep and build knowledge is to integrate it into actions. Stanley Fish, chairman of the Department of English at Duke University, recognizes that cultural literacy "is not a conglomerate of items. . . . It's a whole set of lived practices in relation to which certain things are familiar and known to you. The only way to be culturally literate in any culture is to be a long-term participant."[2] Or, as the old saw has it, "Use it or lose it."

The siege syndrome or "Chicken Little mentality" is a third faulty response to Christian illiteracy. We cannot withdraw the church from the surrounding culture, running in panic because we are overcome by the sheer size of the problem. Nor can Christians simply hide from the growing lack of knowledge, writes philosopher Douglas Groothuis, and "stick their heads comfortably in the sands of ignorance."[3] Instead, we can keep in mind mottoes like these: *No living in an ivory tower. No keeping Christ-centered Christianity in a little Bible box. No talking and not doing. No Sunday-morning Christians—outspoken in the church but nonentities on the job.* When we witness to and "stand by the truths [we] have learned" (2 Tim. 3:14, NEB), that confirms them to our souls.

In sum, education is no cure-all; there are no easy answers, and the church cannot withdraw from the battle. But some strategies that have worked can help the family and church fight the erosion of what remains of the Christian core and begin its rebuilding.

The family doctor says

When physicians want to make their patients better in the long run, they suggest lifestyle changes. So, doctor, what are some prescriptions that can make the state of Christian literacy healthier in our families?

Set priorities. Create a family environment of immersion: This is what the Deuteronomic injunction (Deut. 6:6–7) means when it speaks of teaching the words and commands of God "diligently to [our] children," talking of them when we "sit in [our] house . . . walk by the way, . . . lie down" and rise.

While narcissism was the main descriptor for young people in chapter 6, it isn't just the young, of course, who have the self-centered disease. Editor David Awbrey charges the entire culture with the sickness all too many Christians have fallen into: "America's mass mental illness may be that many of us have lost touch with ourselves, our families, and our friends. In their place, some of us have substituted a mad pursuit of material wealth—an attitude of 'he who dies with the most toys, wins.' "[4] We cannot find the determination to know what we need to know if we are sick with self love; thus, one step in restoring the core of Christian literacy is renouncing the obsession with self.

Eat your daily bread, says the doctor. He knows you must read your Bible every day. Nothing else you can do will make such a difference to your life. It is not by chance that three-fourths of what we think every Christian should know is from the Bible. And it is important to read the Bible through—not necessarily in a year. This is one prescription that cannot sit on the shelf. It should be taken every day. It is important to read Scripture in an organized fashion. One study Bible recognizes that, although most Christians have started to read the Bible through in a year, only a few ever complete it.[5] And well under 10 percent of youth surveyed have "any regular, voluntary habit of Bible reading," many doubting their faith "because they were unable to read the Bible as they thought they ought to."[6]

Memorizing from the Bible will make the daily bread always accessible to you. Memorizing is hard for many, but there are ways to make it easier. The Bible is available on cassette in several versions, so commuters can listen while driving to or from work. And many Scripture passages have been set to music; the melodies make memorizing both easier and more pleasant. Wes Willis of Scripture Press emphasizes word-for-word learning, especially with preschoolers, who "absorb things without even trying. . . . Scripture memorization provides the building blocks that the Holy Spirit will work with later."[7] The young *will* memorize, and if we don't help them fill their minds with truth, those same minds will be filled with garbage—the latest commercials, rock songs, and dialogue from *The Rocky Horror Picture Show*.

Study. Approach the list of terms at the back of this book like a smorgasbord if you would like to get started. At least that can make you aware of some things you may not have known were missing from your diet. Study does not need to be a dull or solitary diet, either. Have you considered taking a class at a local Christian college? Or forming a study group to discuss issues or classics? And there are Bibles and Bible studies of varying quality for computer, on video, and in games.

Know what the essentials of the faith are so that you can respond accurately to the growing anti-Christian charges in our society. Know the Judeo-Christian heritage (law, literature, history) and what it has meant to our nation in order to keep building bridges and keep reminding Americans where they come from. The doctor would tell you: Stubbornly stick to the task of learning more about your faith. Know God's words so well that you can know and do his will, so that you can, in Johannes Kepler's words, "think God's thoughts after him."

Read the right books is a supplementary prescription. Although we have not tried for completeness, you could begin with a very basic diet chosen from the reading list at the end of this book. (For some people, reading lists are a kind of check-up.) Then you can have in your personal library, and suggest for the church library, a balanced diet; for example, do you have right at hand a Bible dictionary, a Bible-study book, a complete concordance, and so on? Do you take time to read at least one Christian magazine that keeps you abreast

There's Something About That Name

Five different ways to spell Jesus.

In the first centuries A.D., many believers did not use the cross as a symbol for Christ. It was still considered the instrument of a low-born criminal's execution. Instead, they used initials and abbreviations as codes and symbols for Christian identity.

Alpha and Omega. In Revelation 22:13, Jesus calls himself "the Alpha and the Omega." These letters, the first and last of the Greek alphabet, are used now as symbols in stained-glass windows. But archaeologists have found the letters scratched in plaster dating from times when it was dangerous to be known as a Christian.

Chi rho. The first two letters of the Greek word for Christ, *chi* (which looks like an X) and *rho* (which looks like a capital P), are often superimposed to form a monogram for the name of Christ. In 1963 archaeologists in Britain excavated a mosaic floor in Somerset containing a portrait of a clean-shaven Christ with the *Chi rho* behind him. This remarkably well-preserved floor, which dates from the fourth century, can now be seen in the British Museum. The *Chi rho* is still incorporated into architecture and art to represent Christ.

Ichthus. The letters of this Greek word for "fish" are an acronym for *Iēsous Christos Uios Theou Sōtēr* (Jesus Christ, Son of God, Savior). Thought to be a secret sign among early believers, in more recent times the fish began appearing in felt banners on church walls as well as on the bumpers of cars belonging to openly evangelistic believers.

IHS. *IHS* (or *IHC*) is often inscribed on altars or embroidered on liturgical vestments. In that setting it stands for the first three letters of the Greek name of Jesus. The *Catholic Encyclopedia* says that "other interpretations of the characters are only pious fancies." Here is one of those pious fancies: According to legend, the Roman Emperor Constantine had his soldiers paint the *chi-rho* monogram on their shields before a battle. This was in obedience to a vision in which he had been promised, *In hoc signo vinces*—"In this sign you will conquer." They won, and thus, according to pious fancy, IHS stands for *In hoc signo*.

INRI. Classic paintings of the crucifixion (and carved devotional crucifixes) often bear the letters INRI on a plaque above the head of Jesus. The letters stand for the Latin *Iesus Nazarenus Rex Iudaeorum*—"Jesus of Nazareth, King of the Jews" which, according to John 19:19, Pilate wrote not only in Latin, but in Hebrew (Aramaic) and Greek.

of current Christian concerns? Do you have a Christian quotation book so you can quote what earlier saints have said on the topic you want to talk about? Have you read the ten or twenty all-time Christian classics?

Healthy families read good literature aloud. That creates readers. We know that one of the main reasons people don't read the Bible is that they don't read much of anything. So if you can make your family into readers, you have won more than half the battle of getting them into the Word. Christian children's books of high quality are multiplying. With so many beautiful and biblically sound ones, why waste time on those that are not the best? (This naturally implies less time spent watching television.) But telling and reading stories is not just for children; it can continue as a communal spiritual experience as long as the family lives together. One mother we know about read to her children until they were in college; to this day, before the family gets together on holidays, her adult children call to request their favorites be brought and read.

Sing, to yourself and with others. Sing for praise and devotion, no doubt, but also for teaching. Buy a hymnbook for singing at home. Helen and David Seamands's family learned what that could mean when serving as missionaries for sixteen years put them far from a support system. Helen says, "One of the most important things we took with us to India was a piano, because I like to play old hymns. I memorized *The Methodist Hymnal* during our time out there and the words of those great hymns became precious to me and the children." David, who was gone out to neighboring villages for weeks, adds, "To this day, when our kids visit we'll gather around the piano to play and sing those hymns. It's an important part of our life."[8] Have you ever tried *reading* the hymnbook, looking up the scriptural allusions often listed there?[9]

Teach might be the an unexpected prescription. But when you teach, you most truly learn for yourself. Family members need to absorb Christian knowledge through their pores. "Religious training at home [is] a key factor in future church involvement," found the Princeton Religion Research Center.[10] Of course, the place you learn a lifestyle is at home. So read and talk the Bible all the time. Children should know Joseph and his brothers like they know their own brothers; they should know the Promised Land like their own land. That is what provides the context that it takes to be a literate Christian later, and it prevents one barrier to Bible reading—a lack of basic, underlying information—from ever being built. Our friend Judy understands that; she wonders, "Why are we throwing away so much of the good old stuff? There is a breakdown in the system. But there's so much God wants parents to teach. Our love is the biggest persuader to Christian knowledge going. Then it's contagious—they catch what *we* have."

That is why we focus so much here on teaching in the family.

Judy counts on the extended family as teachers, too, helping her children grow strong. When you ask youngsters anywhere to tell you two or three people who are central to their lives, they will often say a grandfather or a grandmother. Nez Percé Indians gave grandmothers the task of passing on their culture, because they understood how essential the old are. We can borrow their method when we pass on Christian knowledge:

> Ancient language—pantomime hands—
> Your own people's creation in story and song,
> Not one word, not one movement, must you miss,
> . . . Tomorrow's proof of living past.[11]

Teach discipline as well as content if you are a parent or teacher of children. You may wonder what discipline has to do with Christian knowledge: As the profile of young people in chapter 6 reminds us, unless children learn to obey the parents who model God's love and authority, they won't want to seek God, and won't want to know more about him. Annie Sullivan, the teacher of one of the most famous students of all time, Helen Keller, said, "Obedience is the key to the *mind* of a child."[12]

It is never too early to begin teaching children to feed their souls. Psychiatrist Bruno Bettelheim's *The Uses of Enchantment* explains how very young children select a certain fairy tale to read over and over, and how it shapes them.[13] Christians can recognize a similar process in their lives when they think back about how they have identified with and perhaps unconsciously patterned themselves after a particular Bible character. Poet and abolitionist John Woolman longed for heaven because he read Revelation 22 for himself when he was seven years old; when he was a rebellious teenager, he was brought back to God by some of his earliest experiences of knowing about his Father.[14]

With everything that the family has to teach, and with so many children who are not doing well, Judy worries, "I'm afraid for my children." So she asks the doctor, "With all that's wrong, can I overcome it?"

"I know a woman," the doctor answers, "whose experience shows that even families under siege can do what needs to be done. She found herself single with five children aged ten to sixteen, the very age a divorce makes the most impact. They spent their family time in churchgoing, devotions, and marathon sessions, talking biblical principles day and night. They spent thousands of dollars on Christian high school and Christian college, driving old cars, going without, praying a lot (and eating macaroni and cheese a lot), with the children working in fast-food restaurants to help. Her children are grown now, and all are Christians. She says it was worth it—and she would do it again."

Finally, parental concern for teaching children should not end at the door of your home. Doesn't it go without saying that what your child learns outside your home is your responsibility, too, because you are that child's steward before God? If the situation there is not healthy, consider paying the cost to have your children attend Christian school. This includes Christian college, since college is the usual place for making decisions about what to do in life and whom to marry. Public universities have Christian houses and strong Christian organizations that suit some better, so each parent and child will want to weigh both possibilities. However, even if it is only for a year or two, and even if it is expensive, students who later became doctors or teachers or engineers at other universities often say their start in a Christian college was worth it.

Pray. The old saying is true: "The family that prays together stays together." We believe from experience in our own families and others that reading the Bible and good books and praying together are the healthiest actions a family can take. Have you fostered private Bible and prayer time in other family members? One eager-beaver family began early: They read the Bible to their baby before she was born!

Be a role model. This prescription is like the one to teach; you will learn more and grow stronger when you are accountable. An aging aunt of one of the authors has set as her priority to know Christ; the secret of her spiritual power is that she consistently does what is important (reading the Word constantly, praying without ceasing) rather than being ruled by the tyranny of the merely urgent. She is a pattern for many. But being a model is not only for the old, as Paul told the youthful Timothy (1 Tim. 4:12). Young parents often find that the time they begin to want to know more about Christianity is when they begin to have children because they then want to model well.

What do the children see as the real, the important things in your family? The parents' commitment to the church, as shown by

"Okay, four-year-olds! Let's polish off the Book of Leviticus!"

attending church and by seeking and carrying out church responsibilities? And the parents' esteeming the Bible, turning to it for answers to tough problems? And the parents' commitment of time and energy to the children? Keeping a time log for a week to test those priorities might be a salutary shock to the system.

Join together. The family physician knows that individual patients can often help each other make important lifestyle changes if they get together. If you are single, you need a support group. If you are in a family, think about how to enhance that support group.

This means, for example, eating at the same table at the same time. Feed relationships as well as bodies—and without the television. "Today's dinner hour is no Norman Rockwell painting," Laurence Sombke says of Americans, even though "3 out of 5 of us say we observe the daily ritual" of the evening meal together. "But what are 50 percent of adults doing at dinnertime? Eating with Tom Brokaw and Vanna White, according to a [1988] Roper Reports study . . . which found TV viewership during meals up from 33 percent in 1977."

For years, he says, the evening meal has meant talking, finding out what is happening in one another's lives, and teaching the "social graces."[15] The dinner table is one place Christians have always inculcated manners—and much else besides.

Crucial maintenance for the church

Individuals and then families make up the single organism of the church. Paul's favorite image for the church is Christ's body; its health, as he said, depends on the health of each of its organs (1 Cor. 12:26). Although he did not see the church as a car or chariot, that metaphor will be useful to us. Puritan pastor/poet Edward Taylor wrote of the church as a flying coach carrying the saints: "For in Christ's coach they sweetly sing, As they to glory ride therein."[16]

We, too, like to think of the church as running along sweetly, like a well-tuned car. If we extend the metaphor, we can ask, What does our car need most to run right on the journey of life?

On the outside, the American church is a beautiful, up-to-date model with all the latest gadgets, a shiny finish, and lots of chrome. Looking on the outward appearance, we might question whether the church needs to be brought in for a major overhaul. But keeping a car running is an everyday maintenance job. Let too much go, and it is in trouble. Let too much go wrong, and one day we find the car dead.

If we decide to take the car apart for an overhaul, especially for the sake of Christian literacy, we might first check out *teaching*. Our checklist could read:

- Are all mature members teaching in some capacity, or are some asking others to do the job while they act like missing cylinders?
- Are elders taking care over what is being taught, "holding fast the faithful word" (Titus 1:9, NASB)?
- Do confirmation and Sunday school need revamping so that they truly teach? Eight out of ten Americans attend Sunday school as children—and then half of those become unchurched adults.[17]
- Should we use the International Sunday School Lessons or another system that goes through the entire Bible so that all, even the youngest, learn the Bible in a coherent way? We saw an almost unbelievable film in which babies a few months old were fascinated by God's Word![18]
- Can we provide something like a Christian "Operation Head-start"? This could be an intensive class in which parents, little ones, and teachers work together to teach and learn the biblical lifestyle, both facts and principles. Maybe some parents don't know how and what to teach. Don't we need to intervene on their behalf, even if only a few will begin serious teaching in their homes?
- Do we insure that youth relate with and work alongside older Christians? We have done well to give youth their own program. But does that mean we've made them sit in the back seat? We suggest that young people be integrated into the life of the local church more and sooner. They can learn much from us as they get involved in church committees or work with us as teachers or aides in the Sunday school or nursery.

If our teaching doesn't check out as being in working order, it is no wonder the car slows down.

The church's fuel: Bible reading

The next thing to gauge is whether the fuel is flowing. That means, as we have already said, to *read the Bible,* whatever else the church does.

• Is there leadership in finding ways to help people read the Bible? Writer Tim Stafford says the key is not curriculum (what is being taught), but leadership. He suggests first discovering private Bible reading habits by a confidential survey that asks specific questions like "How many days did you read the Bible in the last week?"[19] If a group goes through the Bible in a year with you, it is easier. (Helpful aids include the *One-Year Bible* or the National Association of Evangelicals checklist.)[20]

• Do you encourage the public reading of Scripture in groups with which you are affiliated—Sunday school, family, Bible study, church? In the Old Testament, this resulted in revival and in covenant keeping: when Moses read the law, and Joshua, and Josiah, and Ezra. Paul told Timothy not to neglect that kind of "public reading" (1 Tim. 4:13, NASB).

• How are Bible-study groups operating? Over the long haul, they make for the best acceleration. Does your small group memorize together from a single Bible version? How do you study? This should not just be the what-does-this-mean-to-you share group, although that is important too. But the car always must be in balance: Sharing cannot be *instead of* rigorous Bible study.

The joyful noise of the coach's advance: Music

Music is an essential accompaniment for joyful traveling, as the poet Edward Taylor reminded us above.

• Does your church sing for teaching as well as worship? Good hymns, such as those of Charles Wesley, teach sound doctrine.

• Does your church sing to memorize Scripture? Such songs were popular in the 1960s and 1970s; some churches still use them. One young man is writing music for his church to sing for its memory verse of the month, which pulls that local body together. Youth groups can learn with the newest musical settings—perhaps even a Bible rap that teaches the books of the Bible.[21]

• Does your song selection help unify your church with Christendom? One Christian friend went around the world and worshiped in English-speaking churches of different denominations. Music was the common ground—everywhere he and his wife went, the congregations sang, "And Can It Be That I Should Gain?" Surprised at the currency of that one song, he saw unity in the new light of "the universal language." The large number of songs held in common is a bond for those who are, after all and regardless of appearances, riding in one car.

• Is music pulling your worship together? Some churches that have traditionally stressed worship are now saying something has been lost there. In open worship, one Quaker said, when not everyone knows the song an older Christian starts, we can't all join in. Youth and their elders are often kept apart by their music in other ways as well. Both groups need to learn the language of each other's music so they can understand it. Communal worship, too, requires communal knowledge.

When a car is screeching, squeaking, and squawking, it needs lubricant. But the more joyful noise of music in worship has through the ages led to Christian fellowship that moves the church forward. We are to teach one another along our journeys, singing as we go in "hymns and spiritual songs" (Col. 3:16). We only have to see the power of non-Christian music to imagine the power it could be for us—no wonder armies in the nineteenth century sang as they fought, and no wonder the armies of Judah marched out with the musicians leading.

Timing: Checking church traditions

Traditional ways to go on the pilgrimage may turn out to be the best yet—tried and true, as people say. Paul thought tradition was important, even though he was not going to make the Gentile church keep all the Jewish traditions: "So then, brethren, stand firm and hold to the traditions which you were taught" (2 Thess. 2:15, NASB). One of the things in which Paul wanted the Corinthian church to imitate him and Christ was "the traditions," which he said they were holding "just as I delivered them to you" (1 Cor. 11:1–2, NASB). So the checklist must include a possible overhaul of the *traditions* your church keeps.

• Has your church made the best use of the symbols it prizes? The church often incorporates symbols—the most central one is the cross, of course. What is surprising is that only a few of the many rich Christian symbols are carried over through all denominations: lamb, palm, anchor, lily, bread and cup, Alpha and Omega, and so on. These in banners, glass, and sculpture enhance worship.

• What about other traditions? Some denominations tend to downplay tradition, thinking that because they do not have a high church liturgy, they have no ritual. But let one such local church change the order of its service, and it will realize how ritualistic it is. All churches have traditions; they simply need to decide which ones are helping them along their way.

• What about liturgy? For many Christians, it continues to have the kind of power a V-8 engine can give. One Episcopalian friend loves the encapsulating of the gospel that she renews in her heart each week just before Communion: "Let us proclaim the mystery of our faith. Christ has died; Christ is risen; Christ will come again." With a program of praise for all church seasons, or music like "A Season to Celebrate," the church can heighten the significance of the yearly cycle.[22] All—even those who do not follow a church year—can do more (and often are doing more) at the high seasons of Christmas and Easter.[23] Some churches and families love keeping very old rituals, such as the first words spoken every Easter Day: "Christ is risen." The invariable answer: "He is risen, indeed."

Thus, for most, the passed-on traditions of their denomination—the words that are used, the way the church looks, the symbols employed over and over—can be inspected and brought back into working condition in the same way that the timing of the engine can be resynchronized. Then those traditions will again carry people along, not hold them back.

The overhaul: Preaching

We should not overlook one major part of the church that may need just a tune-up—or may need a complete overhaul. Ever since Jesus, and especially since the Reformation, *preaching* has forwarded Christians on their journey. Those who preach are urged to give all the counsel of God (Acts 20:27).

Some churches do this, preaching not just part of the Word, but the whole, Old Testament as well as New; preaching not only God's love, but also awe in the presence of a holy God. We don't often, if ever, preach God's judgment; but the fear of the Lord it would remind us of is essential. Proverbs 1:7 explains its relationship to Christian literacy: "The fear of the Lord is the beginning of knowledge."

In many churches the pendulum has swung too far the other way: The preaching is wishy-washy. Seeing that, some churches overcompensate and get stuffy or argumentative, which can itself be a roadblock. When we preach in such dichotomies, we lurch from one side of the road to the other, if indeed we do not fall off.

What makes preaching really go is the telling of the story. The new emphasis on story theology, whether we agree with all its aspects, should remind us of a simple fact: that most of the Bible is God telling us his story. Jesus' example shows stories are not only for children. One reason Easter and Christmas pageants have been popular for hundreds of years is that in them we experience God's story, not somebody telling us about it. Walter Wangerin, Jr., no mean preacher and storyteller himself, recommends that about a sixth of the time preachers should just tell the story (which usually means retelling from biblical narrative) rather than deliver a conceptually oriented sermon. We weep over the broken-up pieces of our culture and our church and ourselves, but Wangerin tells us, "[S]tory causes wholeness. Doctrine may engage the understanding mind but story engages the human whole—body, senses, reason, emotion, memory, laughter, tears—so the man who was fragmented is put together again." Story thus integrates individuals, but it also

> knits peoples into a community whole, in time and across the times. This is what happens when Jews retell and relive the story of the Exodus at Passover, when Christians retell and relive the story of the Passion at Communion. . . . Peoples fragmented are put together again feelingly, in the very hearing of their common story told. This sort of wholeness is not a truth to be learned and preserved; it is itself experience, an event which, when God is believed to participate in it, becomes the Truth that preserves a people.

Is The Story essential Christian knowledge? Yes, indeed, it is at the very heart of the journey. "Please," Wangerin beseeches, "tell the story."[24]

When we preach partially in any of these or other ways, we are contributing to how Christians lack knowledge and how they fail to move forward. But God commands otherwise: "For the lips of a priest should preserve knowledge"(Mal. 2:7, NASB). If Jeremiah were writing today, he might say that spiritual leadership comes from God-given drivers after God's own heart, who will steer "with knowledge and understanding" (Jer. 3:15, NEB). Hosea's prophecy sounds as though it could be made to us: "The Lord has a case against [you] . . . because . . . [of] no faithfulness . . . or knowledge of God in the land"; "[m]y people are destroyed for lack of knowledge" (Hos. 4:1, 6, NASB). D. Bruce Lockerbie joins with us in having

> a favorite moment in the history of biblical instruction, Ezra's reading of the Law while the Levites interpreted it: "They read from the Book of the Law of God, making it clear and giving the meaning so that the people could understand what was being read" (Neh. 8:8, NIV).
>
> If only every professing Bible teacher in schools, colleges, and especially seminaries would heed those words! If every preacher, instead of looking for a catchy topic for this week's sermon, would practice the art of literary explication, the gift of biblical exposition—then perhaps those of us who sit in the pew would not be so biblically illiterate.[25]

Returning to the ancient paths

What can we do about all this? Our culture is very like the one Jeremiah told to

> Stand at the crossroads and look;
> ask for the ancient paths,
> ask where the good way is, and walk in it,
> and you will find rest for your souls. (6:16, NIV)

And our answer has been to call for a return to the old ways. We have said that will create health that floods out from the person to the family to the church to the world, that moves from knowing to doing. The kind of knowing we are talking about does not try to create health by merely injecting culture and learning into the church's bloodstream. The kind of knowing we are talking about is not a sterile intellectualism. Instead, it plainly must take into account the motive of the two most important commands: to love God and to love people (Matt. 22:37–39). It must take to heart the scrutiny of 1 Corinthians 13:2: "If I . . . knew everything about *everything*, but didn't love others, what good would it do?"(LB).

The question now is, on the basis of all we have presented so far, whether we agree that Christian community is essential for the health of individual Christians, that Christian communication on which community depends exists in a much weaker state than we have thought—and that in twenty years, when today's faithful and literate men and women are gone, it could cease to exist at all.

Chapter 8

WHAT WILL HAPPEN?

Writes one reviewer of one of the "what-people-don't-know" studies, "Although Americans are a cheerful and optimistic people, they love to be alarmed, especially when Cassandra scatters graphs, charts, and shocking statistics in her path. Crises are sexy and fun. . . . The latest titillation is the crisis in education; witness the box-office smash of Allan Bloom's book [*The Closing of the American Mind*]."[1]

But an eternally more serious issue is this: What will become of the church in America, already faced with a serious erosion of the core of its Christian literacy? Truthfully, we don't know. But we can imagine a best-case and a worst-case scenario.

Our positive projection can include a thaw or even a spring that begins to melt the crisis away—just the way spring vanquished winter as the precursor of Aslan, the Christ figure in Narnia.[2]

Signs of a thaw are everywhere.

Christian children's literature is burgeoning. Christian music is less derivative and more biblical. We are theologically ready for a change in the face of a dying liberal theology that turned out to be both empty and ineffective.

Some think the current narcissism is an accidental phenomenon and therefore transitory; says one advocate for the homeless, "Listen to the music of Tracy Chapman, of U2. They are harbingers of a shift in mood. . . . I think people have gotten sick of living only for themselves."[3] That is corroborated by the movement toward community, bonding, togetherness, and family, and away from ultraindividualism.

Indeed, yuppies are returning to traditional values, including family and the church. "[C]rushed by the emptiness of having made it, the yuppie is dead. . . . The baby boom[ers] . . . have started to change their expectations," says social forecaster John Elkins. He thinks they will care more about relationships, taking "more time for family, parents, maybe even some of the social institutions, like religion."[4]

As California goes, so goes the nation. And California yuppies are "go[ing] home—to church," proclaims another headline. There is the case of Michael Barlow, who says he had "a classic loss of faith due to sex and rock 'n' roll"; but now every Sunday morning finds him in church, which is "a real tonic." There is the case of Irene Webb, Barlow's wife, who explains, "The church gave us a family, since both of us are far away from our families." And there is the case of Robin Pearse and her fiancé, Tom Drace, who are dropping their current safe and successful occupations to venture out into operating "an inn and spiritual retreat center."[5]

And with their celebrated energy, these redirected yuppies are putting feet to new goals: "In a new survey of people ages 25–45, making at least $40,000 a year, 60 percent did public service work in the past five years and 34 percent gave charity at least a tenth of their income. In their eyes 'doing good' is second only to happy family life as a measure of success."[6] So yuppies are reaching out to others and going to church. It could happen that the rest of the materialistic younger Americans will begin to join them there. And that Christians already in church will become knowledgeable enough about the faith and their needs to answer their deepest questions.

Help could come from another unlikely place: the communications media. Following the lead of Scott Peck and Robert Bellah, professionals in psychology and sociology will offer Christian diagnoses and prescriptions and write of them openly for publishers that are not Christian.[7] Such writings could become even more popular. It could happen that more prime-time television will have scenes like the one on a recent episode of "thirtysomething," in which the climax came when a young man declared, "I believe in God. I didn't think I did, but I do." Some predict television will change as Hollywood shifts out of its atheism "because of the rise of interest in Alcoholics Anonymous that is 'sweeping Hollywood' with the message of reliance on God or 'a Higher Power' for help in getting off booze and drugs," according to writer Dan Wakefield.[8]

It could happen that, partly because the faith is presented with a higher profile and in more convincing detail and greater clarity, the number of believers will continue to grow. There are more claiming to be Christians than ever. A 1988 nationwide survey indicated that the number of those who believed "Jesus Christ is 'God or the Son of God' " as well as those who said they were committed to him, had risen 6 percent over the number making similar affirmations ten years earlier. The same survey "found that unchurched Americans even appear to be more religious than they were a decade ago, which suggests some may be ready to become more regular worshipers." Finally, more children than ever are receiving religious training—in the past ten years the number is up to 69 percent from 60 percent.[9]

So it could happen that the church, with its pattern of knowledge-based *koinōnia,* will draw many, many people in. It could happen that parents, answering God's call to teach their children and grieved or angered at the present deteriorating state of affairs, will turn around their family's lifestyles. So the family, the central institution—and the oldest—for passing along the knowledge of God, could do it again. To do that, the church and the family could work hand in hand. They could better teach God's Word, staking their lives on its permanence and the truth of its promises. In so doing, they could act to change the attitudes and, where necessary, the curricula in the public schools and in the religious training schools their children are attending.

If all the King's horses . . .

It could happen that all the King's horses and all the King's men find they can put the church back together again. That would come about when Christians of diverse denominations become effective in talking to one another. They could really listen, hearing what other persons are saying and understanding it from their own context, and they could really talk, knowing the others are listening. That could weld them together in the Christian unity they are searching for. And that in turn would have come about because they had studied

What Does It Mean To . . .

Scripture is the source of many of our figures of speech. Here are a few—with what they mean and where they come from.

be a doubting Thomas? A skeptic, or someone who will not believe without proof. See John 20:24–29 for the story of how the apostle Thomas would not believe that the other disciples had seen the resurrected Christ unless he placed his hand in the Savior's wounds.

escape by the skin of your teeth? To escape barely, narrowly, with difficulty. Job uses the phrase in 19:20 as the capstone to his catalog of losses. He has lost friends, family, respect, possessions, and health. "I am nothing but skin and bones; I have escaped with only the skin of my teeth" (NIV). Apparently, Job was spared gingivitis.

have feet of clay? To show disappointing weakness of character when people have held you in high regard. See Daniel 2:31–45 for the story of King Nebuchadnezzar's vision of a statue that had a head of gold, breast and arms of silver, belly and thighs of brass, legs of iron, and feet of mixed iron and clay. As the vision went on, the metal got more base.

sell your birthright for a mess of pottage? That's *mess* in the sense of meal (soldiers eat in a "mess hall"), and *pottage* is soup, like the *potage* in French restaurants. The phrase means to trade something of irreplaceable value for something cheap and ordinary, especially something that appeals to the senses. See Genesis 25:33–34 for the story of Esau trading his privilege as the first-born son for bread and "pottage of lentils." The actual phrase is from a chapter heading in the Genevan Bible: "Esau selleth his birthright for a mess of pottage."

and followed the biblical pattern they have in common, and because they have worked to achieve consensus on what language they should hold in common. Many would be drawn to a Christianity that exhibited real unity.

One sign of such unity is cross-denominational Bible studies in neighborhoods. A Southern Baptist future minister's wife said the largest contingent of Christians represented in their small-town Louisiana Bible study was Roman Catholic; this group was hungry to read and study the Word. Another sign is the tendency of many to identify themselves as Christians, not as members of a particular denomination.

It could happen that American Christians will communicate and then fellowship together across racial lines, too, going against the grain of the wider society, particularly as they learn how God wants them to minister to one another. One member of a racially mixed congregation thinks her church "should be the model for more churches."[10]

It could happen that, as families care more about family, adults will care more about younger churchgoers, committing themselves to teaching Sunday school and youth groups. Tapping what Wes Willis of Scripture Press calls the "real resurgence of desire to know the Bible," they will find ways to join fellowship with biblical learning for both teens and adults.[11]

And, as Christians work for closer bonds across the gaps of denomination and race and age, the commonalities of their faith could motivate them to renew the common language. It could thus come to pass that God will answer Paul's prayer, which should be ours: "So we will all at last attain to the unity inherent in our faith and our *knowledge* of the Son . . ." (Eph. 4:13, NEB, emphasis ours).

It could happen that the Holy Spirit also will speak through the Christian knowledge ingrained in our culture. Even with so much loss of Christianity from conscious citation, it is still etched on our unconscious. Why else are television programs called "The Good Samaritan," or a series called "Highway to Heaven"? The Bible is so embedded in us that the names from it are everywhere—our resorts bear names like Paradise Valley or Eden.

And it could happen that if Christian knowledge springs up, morality will be watered and will flourish. The churched yuppies are a moral trickle that could turn into a flood. Writer and movie critic Michael Medved argues for a "reborn sense of ethics" as "one of the pluses of a return to traditional church-going." He says that people "were taught religion with one of the elements missing"—"the 'Thou shalts' "—and that they "want to be made to live up to certain standards." That is why he believes that "New Age beliefs will prove ultimately unsatisfying for many." Those faiths offer "the feel-good transcendence of religion, but with none of the rigor."[12]

So the best case could come to pass, and, in the long run, that could be very good indeed.

The good news about the bad news

Even the worst case may turn out well. Much of this book details the biblical illiteracy that is a pernicious epidemic among the youth. But writer and teacher Virginia Stem Owens was heartened by that bad news—she saw in her students' honest ignorance of the Bible a sign that the culture could start afresh: "[T]he current widespread biblical illiteracy should catapult us into a situation more nearly approximating that of [the biblical writers'] original, first-century audience. The Bible will no longer be choked by cloying cultural associations."[13] Her students' paradoxical fresh shock of recognition is what happens when pagans (or neopagans) meet the gospel.

That is also true of the worst-case situation of continued deterioration and progressivism in public education, once a bastion of Christian and moral knowledge. It will arouse public outcry, says Beverly LaHaye, president of Concerned Women for America. LaHaye asserts,

> America's children are learning values. They are learning that they are free to read books containing verbally pornographic material but it is wrong to read their Bibles. . . . They cannot pray to their Creator but they can participate in hedonistic activities. It is okay to ridicule Christian thought, but do not make judgements regarding homo- or bisexuality or a woman's right to kill her unborn child. . . . If we allow the humanists to maintain control, our public school children will graduate—little more than socialist and humanist ideologues—preoccupied with their attitudes, feelings, and sexuality.[14]

LaHaye calls this "chilling." Yet she says, "I do not believe this vision will become reality—because of [Christians] who will not sit idly by and allow it to [come true] in America."[15] It could happen that humanists who have more zeal for teaching than Christians could carry the day. Or it could happen that public education will once again reflect the majority of Americans in what it teaches.

The worst of the worst

Such is our attempt to look into the future to see as bright a picture as we can. What if we look on the darker side?

The habit of Bible reading may vanish. To understand that trend, we may need to examine the multiplication of Bible versions. Many

"As you can see on your handouts, today's topic is original sin."

have never thought how modern translations could be anything but positive. After all, the faithful, especially among the newer generation of Christians, have often selected, stuck with, and studied one of them; thus the Word is more accessible now. But what a mixed blessing! Most are not reading it. On the other hand, the King James Version of the Bible was a mighty unifier for 350 years of English-speaking Christendom. That exists no more, despite its being, as D. Bruce Lockerbie calls it, "the standard *textus receptus* for all English-speaking and literary-minded readers of the Bible."[16]

Another dark projection is that our Sunday schools may continue their slide into extinction. Some polls have shown enrollment plunging in many denominations, and religion writer Daniel Lehmann of the *Chicago Sun-Times* says adults from the "me generation" attend "encounter" and "fellowship groups," so that "people once counted on to run Sunday morning programs for youth are falling by the wayside." Thus they hinder "the growth of the next generation of adult Christians: the children."[17] Curriculum publishers cater to relevance to the point that little is done well. The curriculum might stay Bible based for a time, but finally that would no longer sell because the few teachers left would decide against using resources that require study from them and their students.

Confirmation could continue on its present course of teaching relevance rather than teaching all the common denominators of the faith; it would merely socialize the young, since public schools will no longer be able to do even that. Youth groups could continue along the path they are on, quickly deteriorating until they are nothing but fun and games. Growing up but not growing in wisdom, young people would pass on even less to their children.

An essential part of the worst-case scenario is that Christians' well-being, will power, and knowledge will erode as America erodes. With its debtor-nation status and shrinking dollar, America will become a second-class nation. The Japanese will rule the world as young Americans drop behind. So the Western world could again become pagan; or the Buddhist and Shinto traditions could come to dominate our culture.

Meanwhile, the family as a cohesive unit disappears. Families more and more rarely eat together. They never talk. They involve themselves during their waking hours at home with television, computers, and electronic games and conveniences, or with drugs, to the exclusion of people. They live side by side, but not together. The essentials do not get passed on.

America's narcissism could end up plunging the country into the chaotic world of *The Blade Runner*, a movie that envisioned Los Angeles as a burning urban jungle, a chaos of robots and violent men. With the increase of drugs and violence, no one would ever go into the unsafe cities, so business would weaken and finally fail. Goods and services would cease. The society would die.

Would physical survival then push out all thoughts of eternal survival? Would the book burnings described in *Fahrenheit 451* then be true about all books, but especially the Bible?[18] Are Israeli kibbutzim right to memorize the Old Testament because of the fear that they will lose the physical books? Could the few surviving Christians be forced underground?

And where would the church have been all this time? First came the loss of the sense of connectedness there, as selfishness and busyness kept adults from serving as leaders and teachers. Then the church lost its sense of tradition because that did not seem relevant to the times. Who cared that Martin Luther nailed up ninety-five theses, or that John Calvin thought the world could be run according to his *Institutes*, or that John Wesley and his followers were circuit-riding preachers, or that William Penn wouldn't take off his hat to the king? Who cared what *Chi rho* or *IHS* or a palm branch or even a cross means? Who cared that we were letting the culture continue to rip away bits and pieces of God's content from our thinking? Who cared that knowledgeable Christians had now passed off the scene one by one?

Then the American church might lose any ability to pull together. Fragmentation would worsen quickly because it would be unchecked by biblical principles. Gone would be our ability to think Christianly in common even *within* a denomination. Other irreparable divisions could follow: over race, economics, age.

The church, now frantic to be relevant, would grab at every fad that came along: anything the culture thought of—monkey see, monkey do. Finally (and this could come sooner than we think), we would not be discernibly different from the rest of the culture, even though it is the world system that Jesus and Paul warned us against.

Christians, dissatisfied with such an unrigorous church but not recognizing the source of their dissatisfaction, would leave the body, leaping into the pseudocommunity of the world. Many uninformed and unknowledgeable Christians would fall into cults or hook up with New Age con men.

An increasing number, particularly the powerless and the ill-taught young, might fall prey to Satanism. And Satanism would grow, wreaking havoc with Christianity. (Already this is happening in many places. A psychologist who works with troubled adolescents in an urban setting says we may lose a whole generation to drugs, sex, and Satanism.)[19]

Philosophically and socially, most Christians could simply drift with the rest of Americans into the "twilight of a great civilization . . . toward Neo-Paganism."[20] We could float sleepily along with the tide until we die for lack of knowledge. Maybe we will keep yawning from crisis overload: We are so tired of doom and gloom. In the end, the salt would be worth nothing, and all that ever was of our Christian culture would be, at best, a faint and mocking memory.

Choosing our scenarios

Will Christian knowledge be passed on? Or will it pass away? That may depend on what people like us determine to do.

We could all enlist in combating the erosion of knowledge. "If we do," says Tim Stafford, "we can expect a church that is alive through Spirit and Word."[21]

Or we could choose to be noncombatants. We can act like Hezekiah and say, Thank you, God, that the judgment will not fall in my time (2 Kings 20:19).

Americans love crises. But they also love to be up and doing—to take action. If we join together, we may be able at least to stem the tide. God only knows. And in the final analysis, God alone can turn the tide.

Appendix 1

WHAT CHRISTIANS SHOULD KNOW: A Preliminary List

We want to say with Paul, "I handed on to you the facts which had been imparted to me" (1 Cor. 15:3–4, NEB). Nevertheless, the list appearing in this appendix is tentative and preliminary; it is intended to exemplify the kinds of knowledge we have found literate Christians share and, we believe, more Christians should share.

We arrived at the list's final form by making it as comprehensive a list as we could (a total of over three thousand items) and then selecting and reselecting until it reached its present size of about eighteen hundred terms. This was done by consulting with others whom we consider faithful and knowledgeable Christians; by consulting with *Christianity Today* editors and Christianity Today Institute Fellows and Scholars; by conducting a limited, informal survey among knowledgeable Christians we know; and finally, by carrying out a more comprehensive survey.

Here are the steps in more detail:

• First, we compiled our preliminary list by brainstorming, consulting concordances and experts, and recording what we heard knowledgeable Christians saying.

• Next, one hundred Christians of both sexes and various ages, geographical locations, and denominations evaluated our preliminary list, ranking items from *most important* to *not important*. (They could also mark *not familiar with the term*.)

• A final survey confirmed our assumption that a core of Christian knowledge does exist and that literate Christians do agree on it. Our respondents were from 750 randomly selected subscribers of *Christianity Today*. Of that number, 351 responded to the survey, or 47 percent, a high response. These are the adults who were the basis for the profile of the literate Christian in chapter 5. The significant point was this: The average respondent understood 88 percent of the items (which were representative of the terms, names, and phrases found in this appendix).

A random selection of five hundred subscribers of *Campus Life* also received a survey; one hundred responded to the survey, or 20 percent, so the assumption can be made that the response is biased toward those who felt more able to answer the questions. (That is, because only one out of five answered, these respondents were somewhat self-selecting and not random.) Even so, the difference between these younger respondents and the older ones is marked: They recognized only 61 percent of the terms. Another way of looking at the data demonstrates the disparity even more clearly, as we have already reported, according to John LaRue of the *Christianity Today* research department: "Half of the terms listed on the questionnaire were understood by 95 percent or more *Christianity Today* subscribers, while only 2 percent of the terms were understood by the 95 percent or more of *Campus Life* subscribers." The median age of these younger respondents was 17.5 years, which makes this study analogous by age to the nationwide random surveys of literacy that have raised such alarm about what young people do not know about history, literature, geography, mathematics, science, and so on.

The dangers of listmaking

As we have explained, our list is only a first-time, preliminary trial. Obviously there will be those who will find *any* list philosophically abhorrent or controversial. Nevertheless, in it we have attempted to include all the kinds of things every Christian should know, including very basic items like *Jesus Christ* or *God so loved the world.* No doubt we invite even more controversy because we want it to be prescriptive, "what Christians should know," not just descriptive, "what Christians do know." That is because Christian faith is not merely optional or merely cultural information.

However, highly literate Christians with whom we have talked do tend to hold in common most of the terms on the final list—in fact, they have a surprising level of agreement. And Christians whom we have surveyed, young and old, tend to agree in an overwhelming way on what we could call the heart of the core of Christian knowledge: the basics of the faith, what one Christian humorously called the *sanctum sanctorum,* a list of a little more than one hundred terms. Therefore, among the terms that follow, we have highlighted in bold type the top one hundred that were almost unanimously agreed upon. Ninety-nine percent of the *Christianity Today* respondents understood these terms; and 90 percent or more of the *Campus Life* respondents understood these terms. In one sense, of course, suggesting one hundred terms as more essential to Christianity than others invites further charges of subjectivism. But we believe readers will be interested to know what terms and phrases are held to be most vital by a sizable number of Christians.

In addition, Christians hold in common many terms that all Americans need to know, as listed by Hirsch.[1] Terms that are on both the Hirsch list and ours are followed by an asterisk.

The encouraging news for the American church is that believers of different ages, sexes, and denominations do have consensus about what the basics are. The consensus held across denominational lines.

But a zone separates the average Christian from the highly literate Christian, a zone composed of terms that literate Christians of whatever age, sex, and denomination tend to know but that average Christians do not know. In this zone we do not find wide agreement; there seems to be little or no consensus about which ones are important. For example, highly literate Christians from nonliturgical churches tend to have some but not complete familiarity with liturgical terms and liturgical church music, whereas average Christians do not; literate Christians also know more contemporary Christian issues, church history, Christian literature, and germane scientific terms than average Christians and, in general, seem to find these more important to their own lives. However, as reported in chapter 6, they are unsure as to whether other Christians need to know these things.

Nevertheless, our bias was toward listing too many rather than too few items on the final list, because, as we have said throughout the book, continually widening breaches between what different groups of believers know, each in our own separate Christian world, will continue to affect the unity of the American church adversely. Hirsch described his grid for selecting terms by, in effect, mapping a country with northerly, southerly, easterly, and westerly borders: "But decisions about many items are not clear cut. The inclusion or exclusion of such borderline items must be matters of judgment; we must draw a northerly border, above which lies specialized knowledge."[2] That would be like our zone that separates highly literate from average Christians.

Hirsch also mapped out "easterly and westerly borderline areas. To the east lie materials that are still too new to have passed into general currency." Along our eastern border, we have been quite cautious, including only a limited number of contemporary terms. However, some will find this is not so extensive and others not so limited as they would like: For instance, we have included on our list fewer current terms or names—*creationism*, for example, but not *contextualize*, or *Desmond Tutu*.

Hirsch's map, finally, included a western border, where the border was drawn just before those "items . . . which have passed from view and are now known only by older generations."[3] Our western border extends further than his; here, too, we have been more conservative in retaining terms, trying to recover some of what is now known only by older generations when we find it valuable in the sense of being classic information that Christians of the past over a period of many years have found valuable. For instance, we have included such less-used terms as *Slough of Despond*, such less-known names as *John Witherspoon* and *Elmer Gantry*, and such archaic phrases as "And with what measure ye mete, it shall be measured unto you." But that is a judgment call on our part; the judgment of other Christians might differ.

Why and how the list should be taken seriously

We agree strongly with Hirsch's view about the objections against such a list, even though some may call ours, like his, "that infamous list." Many similar objections are dealt with in chapter 2. Here we do well to summarize the justification for such a list, and to emphasize the right way of using it.

Hirsch has written,

> There are many things to be said against making a list. . . . Ideological objections to codifying and imposing the culture of the power structure have been among them. These are objections to the whole concept of spreading cultural literacy and are consequently objections to spreading literacy itself, not to making lists. A sounder objection is that the very existence of items it contains will cause students merely to memorize the bare items it contains and learn nothing significant at all. [They] will trivialize . . . information without really possessing it.[4]

Of course, possession is our goal. But when it comes to Christian knowledge, a trivialized recognition of materials would be better than nothing, we think. And memorizing God's Word, for example, however it has been misused or abused, is not trivializing it.

We also are aware that real knowledge, and certainly Christian knowledge, is deeper than the ability to parrot back a mere list of terms, however long. The most important principle underlying any teaching, we believe, is this: "Of course, this curriculum should be taught not just as a series of terms, or lists of words, but as a vivid system of shared associations . . . not just a simple identifying definition but a whole network of lively traits, the traditionally known facts and values."[5]

The best way—and some say, the only real way—people become part of a culture is by learning little by little the shared associations through intensive day-by-day living with them. What Christians need to know can be taught explicitly in a crash course; that is what we believe we must do if we have to—that is, desperate times call for desperate measures. But what we need to know is ideally and biblically taught and caught little by little in a child's growing years at home, at school if possible, and at church.

Thus, the most important caveat is that any list of terms, facts, concepts, and quotations just does not "reflect the true character" of anything.[6] This is especially so of Christianity. Its true character is the reflection of Christ in the Christian himself—his faith in God and his changed life—not what he knows. Although we can't say too often how essential right knowing is to right doing, we stress again that Christianity is a way of life, not a body of knowledge.

A few other comments will help in interpreting the list:

Familiarity with Christian terms, except for those from the Bible, does *not* mean Christians have read that particular literary or historical work. What literate Christians know about the work may have come from other sources: conversation, school, or Sunday school discussion about it, books or magazines that talk about or summarize it, or other sources. One example we have been using is *Pilgrim's Progress*. Literate Christians know the story, but they may or may not have read it; in fact, they may know it simply from a flannelgraph or a short movie version. Average Christians may or may not know any part of the story of this or other Christian classics.

In listing terms, we have sometimes cited as well the common way of saying something, even if that is not an accurate quotation, such as "Pride goes before a fall." Terms are usually only listed once, rather than under several key words. We list many terms, whether they are titles or quotations, just as abbreviated words and phrases. People often recognize the title of a book but know only bits and pieces about it; we draw attention to that by following the term with the word *title* in parentheses. Hymn and gospel-song titles have *(song)* after them. When we are suggesting that Christians should be familiar with the wording of an entire Bible verse or Bible passage, we have put *(text)* after the initial key words.

In the rarer case when Christians should have read and therefore be familiar with an entire piece of literature, we have also put *(text)* after the title; these titles were then included on the reading list. Some of these will be unexpected by many Christians; for example, after the Bible, the best-selling Christian literary masterpiece is Thomas à Kempis's *Of the Imitation of Christ*, which most Protestants haven't even heard of, and which only 62 percent of the literate Christians understood. Here again we have been more prescriptive than some may wish. Although we do not have statistics, we know that a century ago everyone read more of these Christian classics. At that time *Pilgrim's Progress*, Dante's *Inferno* from *The Divine Comedy*, and Milton's *Paradise Lost* were still taught in public school. We listed these even though one difficulty we could not ignore was, as we have already asked, "How can we say to read these classics when most Christians are not even reading the Bible every day?"

Comments appreciated

This is a preliminary list, open to change, if for no other reason than our fallibility.

We also see this as a changing list because, despite our attempts to be conservative on transitory terms, some items are still bound to be short-lived. We said that a number of contemporary ones have already been omitted because they might be too ephemeral. In fact, we were advised not to include most names of Christians who are still alive.

We also see this as a changing list because we surely have left out some items we should have included and included some items we should have excluded; this is unavoidable in a first try.

We will be grateful for all suggestions and other responses, which can be addressed to Dr. Lewis at Friends Bible College, Haviland, Kansas 67059, or to Mr. Palmer at Trinity College, 2077 Half Day Road, Deerfield, Illinois 60015.

Aaron
Abandon hope, all ye who enter here
Abba Father
Abel
Abide in me, and I in you
abolition
abomination of desolation
abortion
Abraham and Isaac*
Abrahamic covenant
Abraham's sacrifice
Absalom
absolution
abstinence
Acts of the Apostles, the
A.D. (Anno Domini)*
A.D. 30
A.D. 70
A.D. 1054
A.D. 1517
Adam and Eve*
adoption
adultery*
Advent
Adventists
Adversary
Advocate
agape
agnostic (agnosticism)*
Agrippa
Ahab
All Creatures of Our God and King (song)
All flesh is grass
All Hail the Power (song)
All power is given unto me
all things to all men
All things were created by him
All things work together for good
All we like sheep have gone astray
Alleluia (Hallelujah)
Almighty
alms
Alpha and Omega*
altar
Am I my brother's keeper?*
Amazing Grace (song)
ambassadors for Christ
Amen
America the Beautiful (song)*
Amish
Amos, The Book of
Anabaptist
Ananias and Sapphira
anathema
And with what measure ye mete, it shall be measured unto you
Andrew
angel
Anglican Church (Church of England, Episcopal Church)*
Annas
Annunciation
anoint
answer a fool according to his folly
anthem
Antichrist
Antioch
Apocalypse*
Apocrypha, apocryphal*
Apollos

apologetics
apostasy
apostle, Apostles*
Apostles' Creed (text)
apostolic succession
Aquinas, Saint Thomas*
archaeology
archangel
Are You Washed in the Blood of the Lamb? (song)
Arius, Arian
ark
ark of the covenant
Armageddon*
Arminian
armor of God
As a man thinks in his heart, so is he
As for me and my house, we will serve the Lord
Ascension
asceticism (ascetic)*
Ash Wednesday
Ashteroth
Ask and it shall be given*
Assyria
Athanasian
atheism, atheist*
Athens*
atonement
Augsburg Confession
Augustine of Hippo, Saint*
Augustus Caesar*
Baal
Babel, Tower of*
Babylon*
Babylonian captivity
Bach, Johann Sebastian*
backsliding (backslider)
balm in Gilead
ban
baptism, baptize*
Baptist*
baptize with the Holy Spirit
bar mitzvah* (bat mitzvah)
Barabbas
Barnabas
Barth, Karl
Bartholomew
basilica*
Bathsheba
Battle Hymn of the Republic (song)*
Be fruitful and multiply
Be not conformed to this world
Be of good cheer
Be ye doers of the word
Be ye therefore perfect, even as your Father . . .
Beast, mark of the
Beatitudes*
Because I live, ye shall live also
Becket, Thomas
Beelzebub (Beelzebul)
Beersheba
Before Abraham was, I am
Before I formed you in the womb, I knew you
before the cock crows
Before they call, I will answer
Behold, I stand at the door and knock
believers' baptism
beloved Son
Belshazzar

Benedict, Saint (Benedictine Order)
benediction
Benjamin
Berea
Bethany
Bethel
Bethesda, Pool of
Bethlehem*
better to marry than to burn
Beulah
beyond this vale of tears
Bible
Bible Belt*
binding and loosing
bioethics*
birth control*
birthright
bishop*
Bishop of Rome
blaspheme (blasphemy)
bless (blessed, blessing)
Bless the Lord, O my soul
Blessed are the meek, for they shall inherit the earth
Blessed are the merciful . . .
Blessed are the peacemakers . . .
Blessed are the poor in spirit . . .
Blessed are the pure in heart . . .
Blessed are they that have not seen and yet have believed . . .
Blessed are they that mourn . . .
Blessed are they which are persecuted for righteousness' sake . . .
Blessed are they which do hunger and thirst . . .
Blessed art thou among women
Blessed is he that cometh in the name of the Lord
blind leading the blind*
blood (of Christ, of the Lamb)
Boaz
body of Christ
bondage
bone of my bones and flesh of my flesh
Bonhoeffer, Dietrich
Book of Common Prayer*
Book of Life
Booth, General William
born again
bottomless pit
Bread of Life
breastplate of righteousness
breath of life
bricks without straw
Bridegroom
bright and morning star
brotherly love
bulrushes
Bunyan, John
burning bush
burnt offering
By grace are ye saved
By their fruits ye shall know them
By this shall all men know that ye are my disciples, if you have love one to another
Caesarea Philippi
Caiaphas
Cain and Abel*
Caleb
Calvary*
Calvin, John (Calvinism)*

Can a leopard change his spots?
Can any good thing come out of Nazareth?
Cana
Canaan
canon
canon law
Capernaum
capital punishment*
Cardinal
cardinal sin
carnal
Cast your bread upon the waters*
casting all your care upon him . . .
catacombs
catechism
cathedral
Catholic*
cedars of Lebanon
Celestial City
celibacy
censer
centurion
Cephas
charismatic
charity (love)
chastisement
chastity
cherub, cherubim*
Chesterton, G. K.
chief end of man
chief priests
Choose you this day whom ye will serve
chorale
chosen people*
Chi rho
Christ*
Christ is risen. He is risen indeed
Christ the Lord Is Risen Today (song)
Christian*
Christian Science*
Christianity*
Christmas
Chronicles, the First Book of the
Chronicles, the Second Book of the
church (Church)
Church's One Foundation, The (song)
circumcision (circumcise)*
City of David
City of God, The (title)
clean heart
cleansing the temple
clergy, clerical
coat of many colors*
collect, the
College of Cardinals*
Colosseum, the*
Colossians, the Letter of Paul to the
Come, let us worship and bow down
Come now and let us reason together
Come unto me, all ye that labor . . .
Comforter, the
commandment(s)
common grace
communicant

Communion
communion of saints
communism*
concordance
concubine
condemnation
confession
Confessions (title) (St. Augustine)*
confirmation
congregation
congregationalists
consecrate
conscientious objector*
Consider the lilies of the field*
Constantine the Great*
consubstantiation
contrite
convert, conversion
conviction of sin
Corinth
Corinthians, the First Letter of Paul to the
Corinthians, the Second Letter of Paul to the
Cornelius
cornerstone
Council of Nicaea
Council of Trent*
Counselor
Counter Reformation*
covenant*
covet
Create in me a clean heart, O God
creation
creationism*
Creator
creed
cross
Crown Him with Many Crowns (song)
crown of glory
crown of life
crown of thorns*
Crucifixion, the (crucify)*
Crusades*
cubit
cult*
cup runneth over
Cyprus*
Cyrus
daily bread
Damascus Road
damnation
Dan
Daniel
Daniel in the lions' den*
Daniel, The Book of
Dante*
Darius
dark night of the soul
Darwin, Charles*
David
Davidic Covenant
Day of Atonement
Day of the Lord
deacon
Dead Sea*
Dead Sea Scrolls
Death, where is thy sting?
Deborah
Decalogue, the
defile
deism*
Deluge, the

demon
demon possession
demoniac
den of thieves
denomination
depravity, total
Deuteronomy
Devil
devotions
devout
diadem
diaspora
Didache
Diet of Worms
diocese
disciple
Disciples*
Disciples of Christ
dispensation
dispensationalism
dispersion
dissenter
divideth his sheep from the goats
Divine Comedy, The (title)*
divine fiat
Do not let your left hand know what your right hand is doing
doctrine
Do unto others as you would have them do unto you* (proverbial version)
dogma*
Dominic, Saint (Dominican Order)
dominion
Donne, John*
Douay version of the Bible
doubting Thomas
dove
Doxology (song)
dross
dualism*
Dust thou art, to dust returnest
earth is my footstool, The
earth was without form and void
Easter*
Eastern Orthodox Church
Eat, drink, and be merry, for tomorrow we die*
Ebenezer
ecce homo (Behold the Man)
Ecclesiastes (or the Preacher)
ecclesiastical
ecumenical, ecumenism*
Eddy, Mary Baker*
Eden, Garden of*
edification (edify)
Edwards, Jonathan*
Egypt*
El Shaddai
elder
election (elect)
Eli
Elijah
Eliot, T. S.*
Elisha
Elizabeth (kinswoman of Mary)
Emmanuel (Immanuel)
Emmaus
empty tomb
Enoch
Enter into his gates with thanksgiving
entertained angels unawares

Ephesians, the Letter of Paul to the
Ephesus
ephod
Ephraim
Epiphany
episcopal
epistle
Erasmus*
Esau's birthright
eschatology
Essenes
established church*
Esther, the Book of
eternal (eternity)
eternal life
eternal security
ethical relativism*
Eucharist
eunuch
Euphrates River*
euthanasia*
evangelical
evangelism, evangelist
everlasting arms
everlasting life
Every valley shall be exalted and every mountain and hill made low
evolution*
ex cathedra*
exalt
Except a corn of wheat fall into the ground and die, it abideth alone
excommunication
exegesis
exhort
exile
existentialism*
Exodus*
exorcism
expiation
expository preaching
extreme unction
eye for an eye, an*
Ezekiel, the Book of
Ezra, the Book of
Fairest Lord Jesus (song)
faith
Faith is the substance of things hoped for, the evidence of things not seen
Faith of Our Fathers (song)
Faith without works is dead
fall of Jericho
fall of man*; the Fall
false prophet
false witness
farthing
fasting
fat of the land*
Father forgive them, for they know not what they do
father of lies
Father of lights
Faust, Faustian*
fear of the Lord
fear of the Lord is the beginning of wisdom, The
Feast of Tabernacles (Booths)
Feed my sheep
feeding the five thousand
feet of clay*
fellowship
fiery furnace

fig tree, parable of the
fight the good fight
filthy lucre
Finney, Charles
fire and brimstone
Fire shall not be quenched
firmament
first Adam
First Amendment*
first-born
1 Corinthians 13 (text)
first fruits
First shall be last
fishers of men
586 B.C.
Flee the wrath to come
fleece, put out a
flesh
flesh and spirit
flock
Flood, the
follow me
fool hath said in his heart, There is no God
For my thoughts are not your thoughts, neither are your ways my ways
For what is a man profited, if he shall gain the whole world and lose his own soul?
forbidden fruit*
foreknowledge
foreordain
Forgive them, for they know not what they do*
Forgive us our trespasses, as we forgive those who trespass against us
forgiveness
fornication*
forty days
forty years
fountain of life
four horsemen of the Apocalypse
432 B.C.
1400 B.C.
Fox, George
Foxes have holes, and birds of the air have nests . . .
Francis of Assisi, Saint*
Franciscan Order
free churches
free will*
freedom of religion*
Freely ye have received, freely give
freewill offering
fresco*
Freud, Sigmund*
friar*
friend who sticks closer than a brother
Friends, Society of*
fruit of the Spirit
fruit of the vine
fundamentalism,* fundamentalist
Gabriel
gain the whole world, and lose his own soul
Galatia
Galatians, the Letter of Paul to the
Galilee
Galileo*

Gantry, Elmer
garment of salvation
gathered to their fathers
Gaza
Gehenna
genealogy
Genesis*
Genesis 1:1 (text)
Gentile*
genuflect
Get thee behind me, Satan*
Gethsemane
giants in the land
Gideon
Gideons International
gifts of the Spirit
gird up your loins
Give us this day our daily bread
giving honor unto the wife, as unto the weaker vessel
Gloria in excelsis Deo
Gloria Patri (song)
glory (glorify)
Glory to God in the highest and on earth peace, good will toward men
glossolalia (speaking in tongues)
gluttony
Go and sin no more
go the second mile
Go to the ant, thou sluggard
God be merciful to me a sinner
God became man
God created man in his own image
God, God the Father
God is a Spirit, and they that worship him must worship him in spirit and in truth
"God is dead" theology
God is great, God is good, and we thank Him for our food
God is love
God is no respecter of persons
God is our refuge and strength, a very present help in trouble
God loves a cheerful giver
God-Man
God Moves in a Mysterious Way (song)
God of Our Fathers (national hymn)
God said, Let there be light; and there was light
God so loved the world that he gave his only begotten son (text)
God willing (Deo volente)
God-shaped vacuum
Gog and Magog
gold, frankincense, and myrrh
golden calf*
Golden Rule*
Golgotha*
Goliath*
Good Friday*
good name is better than riches, A
good news
Good Samaritan*
good tidings of great joy
good works
Gospel*
Gospels, the
Gothic*

grace
grace to help in time of need
Graham, Billy*
graven image
Great Awakening
Great Commission
Great Is Thy Faithfulness (song)
Great Tribulation
Great White Throne
Greater love hath no man than this, that a man lay down his life for his friends
Greek Orthodox Church*
Gregorian Chant
grind the faces of the poor
Guide Me, O Thou Great Jehovah (song)
guilt
Gutenberg, Johann*
Habakkuk, the Book of
Hades*
Hagar
Haggai, the Book of
Hallowed be thy name
Halloween (All Hallow's Eve)
Handel, George Frideric*
handwriting on the wall*
Hannah
Hannukah (Chanukah)*
hard heart
Hark! the Herald Angels Sing (song)
harlot
He that findeth his life shall lose it . . .
He that loveth his life shall lose it . . .
He that is without sin among you, let him first cast the stone
He that spareth the rod hateth his son
He was despised and rejected by men
heap coals of fire on his head
Hear, O Israel: The Lord is our God, the Lord is One!
Hear the word of the Lord
Hearing, they hear not*
heart is deceitful above all things and desperately wicked, The
heart of flesh, heart of stone
heathen
heaven
Heaven and earth shall pass away
heavens declare the glory of God; and the firmament showeth his handiwork, The
Hebrews, the Letter to the
Hebron
hedonism*
heir (inherit)
hell
help in time of need
Her children rise up and call her blessed
Here am I; send me
Here I stand; I can do no other. God help me
Herein is love, not that we loved . . .
heresy, heretic*
Herod the Great
Herodians

Hezekiah
high church
high priest
higher criticism
Hill'el
Him that cometh to me I will in no wise cast out
Hinnom, Valley of
His lovingkindness (mercy) endures forever
His thoughts are higher than our thoughts
Ho! Everyone that thirsteth
holier than thou
holiness movement
Holocaust*
holy (holiness)
Holy Grail*
holy ground
Holy, Holy, Holy is the Lord of Hosts
Holy, Holy, Holy! Lord God Almighty! (song)
Holy Land
Holy of Holies
Holy One of Israel
holy orders
Holy Roman Empire*
Holy See*
Holy Spirit (Holy Ghost)
holy war
holy writ*
homiletics
homosexuality*
Honor thy father and thy mother that thy days may be long
Hope springs eternal . . .*
Hosannah
Hosea, the Book of
house divided against itself cannot stand
How are the mighty fallen!
How art thou fallen from heaven, O Lucifer, son of the morning
How beautiful upon the mountains are the feet of him that bringeth good tidings
How Great Thou Art (song)
How lovely is thy dwelling place, O Lord of hosts!
How unsearchable are his judgments
Huguenots*
humanist (humanism)*
humble (humility)
Huss, John (Hus)
hymn
hypocrite (hypocrisy)
I Am
I am come that they might have life, and that they might . . .
I am that I am
I am the door
I am the door of the sheep
I am the good shepherd
I am the light of the world
I am the Lord, and there is none else
I am the resurrection and the life
I am the true vine
I am the vine, ye are the branches
I am the way, the truth, and

the life
I and my Father are one
I believe in God the Father Almighty (text)
I called, but you did not answer
I came not to send peace, but a sword
I do set my bow in the clouds, and it shall be for a token of a covenant
I go to prepare a place for you
I Have a Dream*
I have fought the good fight, I have finished the race, I have kept the faith
I know that my Redeemer liveth
I thirst
I was a stranger and ye took me in
I will lift up mine eyes unto the hills, from whence cometh my help
I will never leave thee nor forsake thee
ichthus (sign of the fish)
icon
idol (idolatry)
If a man die, shall he live again?
If any man thirst, let him come unto me and drink
If any man would not work, neither . . .
If Christ be not risen, then . . . your faith is . . . vain
If God be for us, who can be against us?
If I forget thee, O Jerusalem . . .
If thou shalt confess with thy mouth the Lord Jesus . . . thou shalt be saved
If thy hand offend thee, cut it off
If ye ask anything in my name, I will do it
If ye love me, keep my commandments
Ignatius of Loyola*
IHS
image of God
Imitation of Christ, Of the (title)
Immaculate Conception*
immanence
immersion
immoral (immorality)
immortal
imputation
In Adam's fall we sinned all
In my Father's house are many mansions
In the beginning God created the heavens and the earth*
In the beginning was the Word and the Word was with God and the Word was God
In the sweat of thy face shalt thou eat bread
In this sign conquer (in hoc signo vinces)
In the world ye shall have tribulation, but be of good cheer
Inasmuch as ye have done it unto the least of these my brethren, ye have done it . . .
incarnate
Incarnation*
incorruptible

Index, the*
indulgences*
inerrancy
infallibility
infidel
inherit the wind
iniquity
Inner Light
Inquisition, the*
inspiration (i.e., of God)
Institutes of the Christian Religion (title)
intercession (intercede)
interdict
Into thy hands I commend my spirit
invocation
Isaac
Isaiah*
Isaiah, the Book of
Ishmael
Israel (nation)*
Israel (person)
Israel shall be a proverb and a byword among all people
It is easier for a camel to go through the eye of a needle than for a rich man . . .
It is finished
It is more blessed to give than to receive
It is not good that man should be alone
It is the spirit that quickeneth . . .
Jacob (Isaac's son)
Jacob and Esau*
Jacob's ladder*
Jacob's well
Jairus's daughter
James, the Letter of
James (the Greater)
James (the Less)
James I (of England)
jawbone of an ass
Jehoshaphat
Jehovah*
Jehovah's Witness*
jeremiad*
Jeremiah*
Jeremiah, the Book of
Jericho
Jericho, Battle of*
Jerusalem*
Jesuit* (Society of Jesus)
Jesus is Lord
Jesus, Jesus Christ*
Jesus Loves Me (song)
Jesus saves
Jew
Jezebel*
Jezreel
Joab
Joan of Arc*
Job*
Job, the Book of
Joel, the Book of
John Paul II, Pope*
John, the apostle
John the Baptist*
John 1:1 (text)
John 3:16 (text)
John, the Gospel According to*
John, the First Letter of
John, the Second Letter of
John, the Third Letter of

John XXIII, Pope*
Jonah and the whale*
Jonah, the Book of
Jonathan
Joppa (Jaffa)
Jordan River*
Joseph and his brothers*
Joseph (husband of Mary)
Joseph of Arimathea
Josephus
Joshua*
Joshua, the Book of
jot and tittle
Joyful, Joyful We Adore Thee (song)
Jubal
jubilee
Judah (kingdom)
Judah (son of Jacob)
Judaism*
Judas Iscariot*
Judas's kiss
Jude, the Letter of
Judea
Judge not, that ye be not judged
Judges, The Book of
Judgment Day*
Just As I Am (song)
just shall live by faith, The
justification by faith*
Kempis, Thomas à
kerygma
keys of the kingdom
Kidron Valley
Kierkegaard, Søren
King James Version (KJV)*
King, Jr., Martin Luther*
King of Kings
King of the Jews (inscription)
kingdom come*
Kingdom, Divided
kingdom is not of this world, My
Kingdom of God (Kingdom of Heaven)
Kings, the First Book of the
Kings, the Second Book of the
Knox, John
koine
koinonia
kosher*
Laban
laity
lake of fire
lamb led to the slaughter
Lamb of God*
Lamb's Book of Life
lamentation (lament)
Lamentations of Jeremiah, the
lamp unto my feet and a light unto my path, a
land flowing with milk and honey*
land of the living
Laodicea
Last Judgment, the
Last Supper, the*
Latter-day Saints*
Law of Christ
Law of Moses
Law of the Lord is perfect
Law versus grace
lay brother
Lay up for yourselves treasures in heaven, where neither moth nor rust . . .

lay reader
laying on of hands
layman
Lazarus and the rich man
Lazarus (brother of Mary and Martha)
Lead us not into temptation, but deliver us from evil
Lebanon*
leaven (unleavened)
lectionary
Lent*
Leonardo da Vinci*
leper (leprosy)*
Let my people go
Let not the sun go down upon your wrath
Let not your heart be troubled. Ye believe in God, believe also in me
Let the dead bury the dead
Let the redeemed of the Lord say so
Let this cup pass from me
Let your light so shine
letter kills, but the spirit gives life, The
Levites (Levi)
Leviticus
Lewis, C. S.
liberal theology
liberation theology
Lift up your eyes and look on the fields, for they are white
Light of the World
light versus darkness
like sheep for the slaughter
like the sand of the sea
lily of the valley
lion of Judah
lion shall lie down with the lamb, The (proverbial version)
litany*
little lower than the angels
liturgy (liturgical)
living water
Livingstone, David
loaves and fishes*
locusts and wild honey
Lord bless thee and keep thee, the Lord make His
Lord gives and the Lord takes away; blessed be the name of the Lord
Lord, have mercy (Kyrie eleison)
Lord, I believe; help Thou my unbelief
Lord is in his holy temple; let all the earth keep silence, The
Lord is my light and my salvation, The
Lord is my Shepherd, the
Lord, make me an instrument of thy peace
Lord of Hosts
Lord shall preserve thy going out . . .
Lord, the
Lord's Day
Lord's Prayer* (text)
Lord's Supper, the
lost coin
lost sheep
Lot's wife*

Love bears all things, believes all things, hopes all things, endures all things
love (charity)
Love covers a multitude of sins
Love is kind
Love never fails
love of money is the root of all evil, The
Love one another as I have loved you
Love the Lord thy God with all thy heart (text)
Love thy neighbor as thyself*
Love your enemies
low church
Lucifer*
Luke, the Gospel According to*
Luther, Martin*
Lutheranism*
Lystra
Maccabeus, Judas (Maccabees)
Macedonia
Madonna, the*
Magi
Magnificat
majesty (majestic)
Make a joyful noise to the Lord, all the earth
Malachi, the Book of
Male and female created he them
man after My own heart, a
Man of sorrows
Man proposes, God disposes*
Man shall not live by bread alone*
Man that is born of woman is of few . . .
Manasseh
manna from heaven*
Man's extremity is God's opportunity
manse
mansions, in My Father's house . . .
Many are called, but few are chosen*
maranatha
Mark, the Gospel According to
Mars' Hill
Martha
martyr
Marx, Karl (Marxism)*
Mary Magdalene*
Masada
Mass*
Massacre of the Holy Innocents
Massacre of Saint Bartholomew's Day
Master
materialism*
Mather, Cotton*
matins
Matthew
Matthew, the Gospel According to*
Matthias
Maundy Thursday
mea culpa*
medieval*
meditate (meditation)
Mediterranean Sea*
meek shall inherit the earth, The*
Megiddo

Melchizedek
Mene, mene, tekel, upharsin
Mennonite*
Menorah
Mephistopheles*
mercy
mercy seat
Mere Christianity (title)
Merton, Thomas
mess of pottage
Messiah*
Messiah (oratorio)
Mesopotamia
Methodism
Methuselah
Micah, the Book of
Michelangelo
Mighty Fortress Is Our God, A (song)
millennium
millstone
Milton, John
minister (ministry)
miracles
missal
missionary
Moab
monasticism
moneychangers
monotheism*
Moody, Dwight L.
More, Sir Thomas*
more than conquerors
Mormon (Latter-day Saint)*
mortal sin, venial sin*
Mosaic covenant
Mosaic Law*
Moses*
Most High
mote in thy brother's eye . . . beam in thine own eye
Mount Ararat
Mount Carmel
Mount Hermon
Mount Moriah
Mount Nebo (Pisgah)
Mount of Olives
Mount Sinai
Mount Tabor
mount up with wings as eagles
Mount Zion*
music of the spheres*
mustard seed
My flesh is meat indeed, and my blood . . .
My God, my God, why hast Thou forsaken me?
My heart is strangely warmed
My kingdom is not of this world
My name is Legion, for we are many
My sheep hear my voice
My soul doth magnify the Lord
My word . . . shall not return to me void
My words shall not pass away
Mystical Body
mysticism*
myth*
Naboth
Nahum, the Book of
Naked came I out of my mother's womb, and naked shall I return
National Association of Evangelicals (NAE)

National Council of Churches (NCC)
Nativity, the*
natural law*
Nazarene, the
Nazareth
Nebuchadnezzar
Negev Desert
Nehemiah, the Book of
neo-orthodoxy
Nero
New Age*
New Birth
new commandment I give unto you, that ye love one another
New Covenant
new creation
New English Bible (NEB)
new heart
new heaven and new earth
New International Version of the Bible (NIV)
New Jerusalem
new man, old man
New Testament*
new wine in old wineskins*
Newman, John Cardinal
next year in Jerusalem
Nicene Creed
Nicodemus
Nile River*
Ninety-five Theses
Nineveh
no creed but Christ
No man can serve two masters*
No man, having put his hand to the plough . . .
No man is an island*
no room in the inn
Noah*
Noachic covenant
Noel*
None doeth good, no, not one
Nor do men light a lamp and put in under a bushel
not what I will, but what thou wilt
Novena
Now abideth faith, hope, love, these three; but the greatest is love
Now I lay me down to sleep
Now is the Son of man glorified
Now Thank We All Our God (song)
Now unto the King eternal, immortal, invisible . . .
Numbers
O Come, All Ye Faithful (Adeste Fideles) (song)*
O for a Thousand Tongues to Sing (song)
O God, Our Help in Ages Past (song)
O Little Town of Bethlehem (song)
O Sacred Head, Now Wounded (song)
O Worship the King (song)
O ye of little faith
Obadiah, the Book of
Of his kingdom there shall be no end
Of making many books there is no end
offertory

oil of gladness
Old Rugged Cross, The (song)
Old Testament*
Old things are passed away
Olivet
omnipotence, omnipresence, omniscience
Onan*
one flesh
1000 B.C.
ontology
ordain (ordination)
ordinance
ordinances, divine
Ordinary
Origen
original sin
orthodox, orthodoxy
Our Father who art in heaven (text)
Our heart is restless until it finds its rest in thee
Our righteous deeds are as filthy rags
Out of his belly shall flow rivers of living water
Out of the abundance of the heart . . .
Out of the depths have I cried unto Thee, O Lord
out of the mouths of babes*
outward and visible sign of an inward and spiritual grace
Oxford movement
pacifism*
pagan
Palestine*
Palm Sunday*
pantheism*
papacy*
papal bull
papal infallibility*
parables*
paradise*
Paradise Lost (title)*
pardon
parish
parochial
parson
parsonage
Pascal, Blaise
paschal lamb
Passion, the
Passover*
Passover Seder
Pater Noster
patience of Job*
Patmos
patriarch
Patrick, Saint
Paul, Saint (Saul)*
pax romana*
Peace, be still
Peace be to you
Peace I leave with you, my peace I give unto you: not as the world . . .
peace like a river
peace of God which passes all understanding, the
pearl of great price*
pearls before swine*
pearly gates
penance
Peniel (Penuel)
penitence

Penn, William*
Pentateuch
Pentecost
Pentecostal
Persia
Peter, Saint* (Simon Peter)
Peter, the First Letter of
Peter, the Second Letter of
Peter's denial
Petra
Pharaoh*
Pharisees*
Philemon, the Letter of Paul to
phileo
Philip
Philippi
Philippians, the Letter of Paul to the
Philistines*
Pietà*
Pietism
piety (pious)
Pilate, Pontius*
Pilgrim's Progress (title)*
pilgrims*
pillar of fire
plagues of Egypt*
platonism
played the harlot
pluralism*
Plymouth Colony*
polemics
polygamy*
polytheism*
Pool of Siloam
Pope, the*
pornography*
postlude
postmillennial
Potiphar/Potiphar's wife
potter and the clay, the
potter's field (aceldama)
Practice what you preach*
pragmatism*
Praise God from whom all blessings flow
Praise to the Lord, the Almighty (song)
Pray for the peace of Jerusalem
preacher
Precious in the sight of the Lord is the death of his saints
predestination*
prelude
premillennial
Prepare ye the way of the Lord
Presbyterian*
presbytery
Pride goeth before destruction (commonly, before a fall)*
priest*
primate*
prince of darkness
Prince of Peace
prince of this world
prochoice, prolife
Prodigal Son, the*
progressive revelation
Prohibition*
Promised Land*
prophecy (prophesy, prophet)
prophet is not without honor except in his own country, A
prophet like unto Moses, a
propitiation
proselyte (proselytize)

Protestant*
Protestant ethic (work ethic)*
Prove all things; hold fast . . .
Proverbs, the
providence, divine*
psalm (psalter)
Psalm 1 (text)
Psalm 23 (text)
Psalm 100 (text)
Psalm 150 (text)
Psalms, the
psaltery
publican(s) and sinner(s)
pulpit
Pure religion and undefiled before God and the Father is this
purgatory*
purify, purification
Puritan*
purity (purification)
Put not your trust in princes
Quakers (Society of Friends)*
quick and the dead
Qumran
rabbi*
race is not always to the swift, nor the battle to the strong, The
Rachel
racism*
Rahab
rain falls on the just and the unjust, The
ransom
Raphael*
Rapture, the
reaping where you have not sown
Rebecca
Red Sea*
reconcile (reconciliation)
reconciliation, ministry of
Red Sea (parting of)*
redeem (redemption, Redeemer)
Reformation, the*
refuge, cities of
regeneration
Rehoboam
Rejoice, and again I say rejoice
Religion is the opium of the people . . .
Rembrandt*
Remember the sabbath day, to keep it holy
remission of sins
remnant
Renaissance*
Render unto Caesar the things which are Caesar's; and unto God the things . . .*
repent
reprobate
requiem*
requiescat in pace (R.I.P)* (rest in peace)
responsive reading
restitution
Resurrection, the*
revelation
Revelation to John, the (Apocalypse)*
reverence (reverent)
Revised Standard Version (RSV)
revival*

right to life
righteous (righteousness)
righteous shall flourish like the palm tree, The
Rise! Take up thy bed and walk
river of God, The
river of life
road to hell is paved with good intentions, The*
robe of righteousness
robe washed white
Rock (Christ, Peter)
Rock of Ages, Cleft for Me (song)
rod of correction
Roman Catholic Church*
Roman empire*
Romans
Romans, the Letter of Paul to the
Romans 3:23 (text)
Romans 6:23 (text)
Romans 8:28 (text)
Rome*
rosary
Rose of Sharon
Rosh Hashanah*
Russian Orthodox Church
Ruth, the Book of
sabbatarian
Sabbath, the*
sackcloth and ashes
sacrament*
sacred
sacrifice
sacrilegious (sacrilege)
Sadducees
Saint Peter's Church*
saints
Salem witch trials*
Salome*
salt of the earth*
salvation*
Salvation Army*
salvation, helmet of
Samaria (Samaritans)
Samson and Delilah*
Samuel
Samuel, the First Book of
Samuel, the Second Book of
sanctify (sanctification)
Sanctify them through thy truth . . .
sanctuary
sanctum sanctorum*
sanctus (holy, holy, holy)
Sanhedrin
Sarah
Satan*
Satan worship
Saul (King)
Savior
scapegoat
Scarlet Letter, The (title)*
scarlet woman*
schism*
scribes
Scripture, Scriptures
Schweitzer, Albert*
Scopes trial*
Sea of Galilee
Search the scriptures; for in them ye think ye have eternal life
second Adam
second birth
Second Coming, the*

sect, sectarian*
secular, secularism*
secular humanism
see through a glass darkly
seed
Seek and ye shall find; knock . . .
Seek my face
Seek ye first the kingdom of God
Seek ye the Lord while he may be found
Semitic*
separation of church and state*
separatists
Septuagint
sepulcher
seraphim
Sermon on the Mount* (text)
Serpent, the*
Seth
Seven Churches of Revelation
seven deadly sins*
722 B.C.
seven last words of Jesus
seven sacraments
seven years of plenty
Seventh-day Adventist*
Shadrach, Meshach, and Abednego
shalom*
sharper than a two-edged sword
Sheba, Queen of*
Shechem
sheol
Shiloh
shepherd (sheep)
shibboleth*
shield of faith
Shrove Tuesday
Sidon
sign of the cross*
Silas
Silent Night (song)*
Simon the Zealot
Simeon
Simons, Menno
sin (sinner)
Sinai*
Sing a new song
Silver and gold have I none, but such as I have . . .
Sistine Chapel*
situational ethics
skin of one's teeth*
Slough of Despond*
Smith, Joseph
social gospel
Sodom and Gomorrah*
soft answer turns away wrath, A*
sola fidei (by faith alone)
sola gratia (by grace alone)
sola scriptura (scripture alone)
soli deo gloria (to God alone be the glory)
Solomon*
Solomon in all his glory was not arrayed like one of these
Son of God
Son of Man
Song of Solomon, the (or Song of Songs)
soul
sounding brass or tinkling cymbal

sovereignty of God
spirit indeed is willing, but the flesh is weak, The
Spirit of the Lord
spiritual (spirituality)
spiritual direction
spiritual songs
spiritualism
Spurgeon, Charles
stand in the gap
star of David
Stephen
stewardship
stiffnecked people
still, small voice
stone which the builders refused is become the headstone of the corner, The
strain at a gnat and swallow a camel*
Strait is the gate and narrow is the way that leads to life
streams in the desert
stumbling block
suffer fools gladly*
Suffer the little children to come unto me, and forbid them not
Suffering Servant
Sufficient unto the day is the evil thereof
Sunday, Billy
Sunday school
supplication
Surely He hath borne our griefs and carried our sorrows
sursum corda (lift up your hearts)
swaddling clothes
Swing Low, Sweet Chariot (song)*
sword of the Spirit
swords into plowshares
synagogue*
syncretism
synod
Syria*
Tabernacle
table (tablet) of the heart
Take up thy bed and walk
talents, parable of the
Talmud*
tares
Tarsus
televangelism
temple*
temple of the living God
tempt (temptation, tempter)
tempted like as we are
Ten Commandments, the (text)*
ten lepers
Tenebrae
tentmaker ministry
Teresa, Mother
testament
testify (testimony)
Thaddaeus
thanks (thanksgiving)
theistic evolution
Then shall the dust return to the earth
theocracy
theology
There but for the grace of God go I

There is a time to be born and a time to die*
There is a way which seemeth right unto a man, but the end thereof are the ways of death
There is none that doeth good, no, not one
There is nothing new under the sun*
There will be more joy in heaven over one sinner who repents than over ninety-nine righteous . . .
Therefore shall a man leave his father and his mother and shall cleave . . .
These are written that ye might believe that Jesus is the Christ
These ought ye to have done, and not to leave the other undone
Thessalonians, the First Letter of Paul to the
Thessalonians, the Second Letter of Paul to the
Thessalonica
They are without excuse
They have their reward
They shall know I am the Lord
They that take the sword shall die by the sword
They that wait upon the Lord shall renew their strength
thief in the night
thirty pieces of silver*
Thirty Years War*
This is my beloved Son
This is the day that the Lord has made
Thomas, the apostle
Thou art the Christ, the son of the living God
Thou art worthy, O Lord, to receive glory and honor and power
Thou shalt have no other gods before me
Thou shalt not bear false witness against thy neighbor
Thou shalt not commit adultery
Thou shalt not covet
Thou shalt not kill
Thou shalt not make unto thee any graven image
Thou shalt not steal
Thou shalt not take the name of the Lord thy God in vain
Though he slay me, yet will I trust in him
though I speak with the tongues of men and of angels, and have not love
Though your sins be as scarlet, they shall be as white as snow
throne of God
throw to the lions*
Thy faith hath made thee whole
Thy will be done
Tiberias
Timothy, the First Letter of Paul to
Timothy, the Second Letter of Paul to
tithe
Titus, the Letter of Paul to
To everything there is a season

To God Be the Glory (song)
To have and to hold from this day forward, for better, for worse
To obey is better than sacrifice
To whom much is given, of him much will be required
To whom shall we go? Thou hast the words of eternal life
Today shalt thou be with me in paradise
Torah, the*
tradition of the elders
Train up a child in the way he should go, and when he is old . . .
transcendence
Transfiguration, the
transgression (transgressor)
transubstantiation
Trappist monks*
Tree of knowledge/life
trees of the field will clap their hands, The
trespass (debt)
tribulation
Tribulation, the Great
Trinity, trinitarian
Triumphal Entry
triune immersion
Truly this was the Son of God
Trust in the Lord with all your heart
turn the other cheek*
Twenty-third Psalm* (text)
twinkling of an eye
two-edged sword
Tyndale, William
Tyre
unction
Underground Railroad*
Unitarian Church*
United Kingdom (Israel and Judah)
unleavened bread
upper room
usury*
Uzziah
valley of decision
valley of the shadow of death*
Vanity Fair
vanity of vanities
Vatican, the*
Vatican II*
veil of the temple
Vengeance is mine; I will repay, saith the Lord
vespers
Via Dolorosa (Way of Sorrows)
vineyard
virgin birth
Virgin Mary*
voice as the sound of many waters
voice of one crying in the wilderness
Vulgate Bible*
wages of sin is death, The
Wailing (Western) Wall*
wait on the Lord
Waldo, Peter (Waldensians)
Walk by faith, not by sight
walk on water*
walking in the light
wandering in the wilderness
Watch and pray

watchman on the wall
watchtower
Watts, Isaac
way of all flesh, the
way of the wicked
way, the
We are his workmanship
We have left undone those things we ought to have done
We ought to lay down our lives for the brethren
We praise Thee, O God (Te Deum laudamus)
weaker vessel
weeping, wailing, and gnashing of teeth
weighed in the balance*
Well done, thou good and faithful servant
well of water springing up into everlasting life
Wesley, Charles
Wesley, John
Westminster Abbey
Westminster Catechism
Westminster Confession
What hath God wrought?
What is man . . .
What is truth?
What therefore God has joined together, let not man put asunder
Whatsoever a man soweth, that shall he also reap
Whatsoever things are true . . . think on these things
When I Survey the Wondrous Cross (song)
When I was a child, I spake as a child but when I became a man . . .
When the Spirit of truth is come, he will guide you into all truth
Where the Spirit of the Lord is, there is liberty
Where there is no vision, the people perish
Where two or three are gathered together in my name, there I am
white as snow
Whither thou goest, I will go, and where thou lodgest, I will lodge
Who is my neighbor?
Who is this that darkeneth counsel by words without knowledge?
Whoever shall say unto this mountain, be thou removed . . .
whole counsel of God
Whom shall I send? And who will go for us?
whom the Lord loves he chastens
Whosoever shall call upon the name of the Lord shall be saved
Wide is the gate and broad is the way that leads to destruction
widow's mite
wilderness
Williams, Roger*

wind bloweth where it listeth, The
wine is a mocker
wine that maketh glad the heart . . .
Winthrop, John
wisdom of this world is foolishness, The
wise as serpents and harmless as doves
Wise Men
Witch of Endor
With God all things are possible
Witherspoon, John
without blemish
Without me ye can do nothing
witness(es)
Wittenberg
Woe is me for I am undone
Woe unto you, scribes and Pharisees, hypocrites!
woman at the well
Women's Christian Temperance Union (WCTU)*
Wonderful Counselor, Mighty God, Prince of Peace
Word of God
word of knowledge
Word of life
World Council of Churches (WCC)
world, the flesh, and the devil, the
worm shall not die
worship
Worship the Lord in the beauty of holiness
wrath of God
Wycliffe, John
Yahweh (YHWH)
Ye are my friends, if ye do whatsoever I command you
Ye call me Master and Lord; and ye say well; for so I am
You cannot serve God and mammon*
Ye have not chosen me, but I have chosen you
Ye must be born again
Ye shall be witnesses unto me both in Jerusalem and in all Judea
Ye shall know the truth, and the truth shall make you free
Ye shall receive power, after that the Holy Ghost is come upon you
yoke is easy, My
Yom Kippur*
You have the poor always with you
You meant it for evil, but God meant it for good
You will go out with joy
Young men shall see visions, and your old men shall dream dreams
Young Men's (Women's) Christian Association (YMCA, YWCA)
Zacchaeus
zealots
Zechariah, the Book of
Zephaniah, the Book of
Zerubbabel
Zwingli, Ulrich

Appendix 2

SUGGESTED READING LIST

A reading list is bound to be criticized.

First, there are those who will disagree with any list. As author Allan Bloom says, "One needn't set up a canon of books to read. In fact, I think such lists are rather silly. The important thing is to find one book and follow where it leads. In that way, a whole world can be constructed that moves from philosophy to literature, art and music. If you touch the heart with one book, it can transform a life."[1]

Second, there are those who will naturally deplore the omission of their favorite books.

Third, there are those who will get discouraged if the list is too long or will feel cheated if it's too short.

But our idea here is to get you started. One way is to prioritize.

Outside of the Bible, we have marked with a double asterisk (**) only a dozen books—some very short—that we believe should be read by every Christian and therefore considered basic for everyone's library. Another group of more than thirty, marked with a single asterisk (*), we find important. After that, the suggestions are more than likely for advanced or avid readers. Many of these works are available in various editions. Purists may be bothered by abridged books, or by the rendering of a classic in modern language, but we hope you will find editions that are both understandable and enjoyable. The important thing is to spend time with the great minds and spirits who have gone before us in the faith.

The Bible, of course

**The first and most crucial book to read is, of course, the Bible. A couple of the most popular modern translations are the New International Version and the New American Standard Bible.

If you want to go through the Bible in one year, the *One-Year Bible* (available from Tyndale House) is laid out for that (don't try to take it to church to follow along, though, since the books are not in the usual order), and the National Association of Evangelicals issues annual bookmarks with a one-year Bible reading plan.

Classics (Nonfiction):

Many of these classics are in print in several editions. We recommend that you talk with a knowledgeable bookseller about an edition best suited for your needs.

**Zundel, Veronica, comp. *Eerdmans' Book of Christian Classics*. Grand Rapids, Mich.: Eerdmans, 1985. Includes selections from *The Didache*, Eusebius, Augustine, Bernard, Thomas Aquinas, Thomas à Kempis, Luther, Calvin, George Herbert, Pascal, Law, Edwards, John Wesley, Kierkegaard, Barth, C. S. Lewis, Merton, and many others. The selections are brief.

Pre-Christian and Early Christian era:

**Augustine. *Confessions.*

__________. *City of God.*

Boethius. *The Consolation of Philosophy.* Trans. Richard H. Green. New York: Bobbs-Merrill, 1962.

The Didache. A second-century "manual" on discipleship.

*Eusebius. *The History of the Church from Christ to Constantine.* Trans. G. A. Williamson. New York: Penguin, 1981.

Plato. *Republic.*

Medieval:

Bernard of Clairvaux. *On Loving God: Selections from Sermons by St. Bernard of Clairvaux.*

*Francis of Assisi. *Little Flowers of Saint Francis.*

Julian of Norwich. *Revelations of Divine Love.* Ed. Roger L. Roberts. Wilton, Conn.: Morehouse, 1982.

**Thomas à Kempis. *Of the Imitation of Christ.*

*Thomas Aquinas. *Summa Theologica.*

Reformation and Seventeenth Century:

*Calvin, John. *Institutes of the Christian Religion.*

John of the Cross. *The Dark Night of the Soul.*

Fox, George. *The Journal of George Fox.*

Foxe, John. *Foxe's Book of Martyrs.*

Brother Lawrence. *The Practice of the Presence of God.*

Luther, Martin. *The Bondage of the Will;* selections from *Table Talk.*

________. *Selections from His Writings.* Ed. John Dillenberger. New York: Doubleday, 1958.

Pascal, Blaise. *Pensées [Thoughts].*

Eighteenth and Nineteenth Centuries:

One good way to own classic selections is to buy used college literature texts. An American literature text would give you selections from Edwards, Cotton Mather, Woolman, T. S. Eliot, etc. An English literature text would give you *Everyman, Piers Plowman, Second Shepherds' Play*, Newman, Donne, Herbert, Spenser, etc.

Edwards, Jonathan. *Selected Writings of Jonathan Edwards.* Ed. Harold P. Simonson. New York: Ungar, 1970.

Finney, Charles G. *Revival Lectures.* Old Tappan, N.J.: Revell, n.d.

Kierkegaard, Søren. *Christian Discourses.* Trans. W. Lowrie. Princeton, N.J.: Princeton University Press, 1971.

Law, William. *A Serious Call to a Devout & Holy Life.*

Mather, Cotton. *Magnalia Christi Americana: Or the Ecclesiastical History of New England.* Ed. Raymond J. Cunningham. New York: Ungar, 1971.

Newman, John Henry. *Apologia Pro Vita Sua.*

Smith, Hannah Whitall. *The Christian's Secret of a Happy Life.* Old Tappan, N.J.: Revell, 1870, 1942.

*Taylor, Howard, and Mary G., *Hudson Taylor's Spiritual Secret.* Chicago: Moody, n.d.

Tolstoy, Leo. *My Confession* (sometimes translated as *My Religion* or *What I Believe*).

Wesley, John. Read from his *Journal* or sermons.

Woolman, John. *The Journal of John Woolman.*

Twentieth Century:
Who's to say what's a classic from our own century? Only those from the next century would know that. So this list is more idiosyncratic, including some just because they're popular.

Carmichael, Amy. *If.* Fort Washington, Pa.: Christian Literature, 1966.

Chambers, Oswald. *My Utmost for His Highest.* New York: Dodd, Mead, 1935.

Chesterton, G. K. *Orthodoxy.* Garden City, N.Y.: Doubleday, 1959.

Cowman, Mrs. Charles. *Streams in the Desert.* Vol. 1. Grand Rapids, Mich.: Zondervan, 1986.

Eliot, T. S. *The Idea of a Christian Society.* New York: Harcourt, Brace, and Company, 1940.

Kelly, Thomas R. *A Testament of Devotion.* New York: Harper & Row, 1941.

**Lewis, C. S. *Mere Christianity.* Rev. ed. New York: Macmillan, 1952. He is our favorite author. Many Christians have read every word of his they can get their hands on—even though that is a great deal. We do not attempt to list all those here.

__________. *Surprised by Joy: The Shape of My Early Life.* San Diego: Harcourt Brace, 1966.

*Merton, Thomas. *The Seven Storey Mountain.* San Diego: Harcourt Brace, 1978.

*Packer, J. I. *Knowing God.* Downers Grove, Ill.: InterVarsity, 1973.

Phillips, J. B. *Your God Is Too Small.* New York: Macmillan, 1953.

*Tozer, A. W. *The Pursuit of God.* Tulsa, Okla.: Christian Publishing, 1982.

Classics (Fiction, Drama, and Poetry)

Medieval:
**Dante Alighieri. *The Divine Comedy: Inferno, Purgatorio, Paradisio*. If you read only one, it should be *The Inferno*. Try to find the edition with Gustave Doré's illustrations: *The Divine Comedy: The Inferno, Purgatorio and Pardiso*. Trans. Lawrence Grant White. Illus. Gustave Dore. New York: Pantheon, 1948.

**Everyman*.

Langland, William. *Piers Plowman.*

Mystery Plays (English). If you want a modern adaptation, try the one that was such a success on the London stage: Harrison, Tony. *The Mysteries*. London: Faber, 1985.

Pearl.

Sir Gawain and the Green Knight.

Renaissance:
**Our favorite poetry collection (includes traditional as well as modern):
Meeter, Merle, ed. *Country of the Risen King*. Grand Rapids, Mich.: Baker, 1978. Poems from Donne, Herbert, Milton, Hopkins, Rossetti, Eliot, Luci Shaw, etc.

**Bunyan, John. *Pilgrim's Progress.*

*Donne, John. "Batter My Heart" and "Death, Be Not Proud" are his best-known Holy Sonnets; these and "Meditation XVII" ("No man is an island") should be known by every Christian—but then, we are prejudiced: Donne is the favorite poet of one of the authors.

Herbert, George. "Easter Wings" and "Love (III)" are the best-known poems.

Marlowe, Christopher. *The Tragedy of Dr. Faustus.*

**Milton, John. *Paradise Lost.* Often recommended: Books I, II, IX, and XII.

Shakespeare, William. Although these plays are not Christian in intent, many believers find the uncut *Hamlet* and *Measure for Measure* to have strong, explicit and implicit Christian values.

*Spenser, Edmund. Selections from *The Faerie Queene.*

Eighteenth and Nineteenth Centuries:
Defoe, Daniel. *Robinson Crusoe.* Abridged versions truncate the Christian emphasis.

Dostoevski, Fyodor. *Crime and Punishment.*

__________. *The Brothers Karamazov.*

Goethe, Johann Wolfgang von. *Faust.* This raises the right questions and gives the wrong answers.

Hawthorne, Nathaniel. *The Scarlet Letter.*

*Hopkins, Gerard Manley. "Pied Beauty," "God's Grandeur," and "The Windhover" are his best-known poems.

Hugo, Victor. *Les Miserables.*

Melville, Herman. *Moby Dick.* Although this is not a Christian book, its questions will intrigue. *Billy Budd* does also.

Rossetti, Christina. "Good Friday" and "A Christmas Carol" ("In the bleakmidwinter") are her most popular poems.

Sheldon, Charles M. *In His Steps.*

*Thompson, Francis. "The Hound of Heaven."

Tolstoy, Leo. His autobiographical conversion is fictionalized and excellently portrayed in the character Lenin in *Anna Karenina.*

__________. *The Death of Ivan Ilych.* Often read by those who deal with death.

__________. *Master & Man & Other Parables & Tales.*

__________. *Resurrection.*

Wallace, Lew. *Ben-Hur.* New York: Harper, 1880.

Twentieth Century:
*Anouilh, Jean. *Becket, or the Honor of God.* Trans. Lucienne Hill. New York: Coward, 1960. (Enjoy the movie version.)

*Auden, W. H. *For the Time Being.* Excerpted in Meeter, q.v.

*Bolt, Robert. *A Man for All Seasons.* New York: Vintage Books, 1962. Biographical drama of Sir Thomas More.

*Eliot, T. S. "Journey of the Magi." Also *Four Quartets,* "Ash Wednesday," *Murder in the Cathedral.*

Greene, Graham. *The Power and the Glory.* New York: Viking, 1946.

*Lewis, C. S. *The Screwtape Letters.* New York: Macmillan, 1946.

Miller, Calvin. *The Singer.* Downers Grove, Ill.: InterVarsity, 1975. An imaginative retelling of the gospel story. This doesn't bear up under frequent rereadings as well as some, but many students are galvanized by it.

*O'Connor, Flannery. *The Violent Bear It Away*. New York: Farrar, 1960.

*__________. *Complete Short Stories*. New York: Farrar, 1971. The most popular story is "A Good Man Is Hard to Find"; "Greenleaf" is also popular (and difficult); "Revelation" is very accessible.

Sayers, Dorothy. *The Man Born to Be King*. London: V. Gollancz, 1943. A drama of Christ.

Shaw, Luci. Some call her our best contemporary Christian poet. Our favorite poems include "To a Christmas Two-Year-Old," "Royalty,' "The Sighting," "Rib Cage."

*Tolkien, J. R. R. *The Lord of the Rings*. New York: Ballantine, 1978, 1981. (Three volumes.)

*Wangerin, Walter, Jr. *The Book of the Dun Cow*. New York: Harper, 1978. This was written for children and won a children's award but is not accessible to most (even older children). Adults often find it deeply moving and class it with Lewis's and Tolkien's fantasics.

*Waugh, Evelyn. *Brideshead Revisited*. Boston: Little, 1982.

Weil, Simone. *Waiting for God*. New York: Harper & Row, n.d.

*Williams, Charles. *All Hallow's Eve*. Darby, Pa.: Arden Lib., 1965.

Children's Books:

Here are some personal favorites, a sampling of what is available. Remember that children's books are for adults, too! Buy the best you can afford; many award-winning books are available in inexpensive paperback.

Nonfiction:
**The most important single book would be a solid Bible story book. You will want several to read aloud. One of the most enduring favorites for you to read to the youngest:

*Taylor, Kenneth N. *The Bible in Pictures for Little Eyes*. Chicago: Moody, 1956.

Jones, Jessie Orton. *Small Rain.* New York: Viking, 1949. Illustrates selected Bible verses. An honor book for the coveted Caldecott illustrator's award.

Poortvliet, Rien. *Noah's Ark*. New York: Abrams, 1986. If you are willing to spend the money on it, we think this huge, beautiful coffee-table book is the best Noah's ark book in the world.

Tudor, Tasha. *And It Was So*. Louisville, Ky.: Westminster, 1988. Uses the Bible words of creation; has been re-released. Tudor is an excellent illustrator of Bible passages for children.

Winthrop, Elizabeth, adapted by. *He Is Risen: The Easter Story*. Illus. Charles Mikolaycak. New York: Holiday, 1985.

Other Nonfiction:
Hunt, Gladys. *Honey for a Child's Heart*. Grand Rapids, Mich.: Zondervan, 1978. This is a book for Christian parents about reading for children.

Macaulay, David. *Cathedral: The Story of Its Construction*. Boston: Houghton Mifflin, 1973. Honor book for the Caldecott.

Fiction:
Beware of abridged versions of children's classics.

Bianco, Margery Williams. *The Velveteen Rabbit.* Available in many editions, some with audio cassette.

Burnett, Frances Hodgson. *The Secret Garden.* New York: Dell, 1980.

*L'Engle, Madeleine. Her science fiction trilogy is the most popular, with *A Wrinkle in Time* (New York: Dell, 1962) winning the coveted Newbery award for the best children's book of the year. The others in the series are *A Swiftly Tilting Planet, Many Waters,* and our favorite, *A Wind in the Door.* Her realistic Austin family series is also wholesome and well written.

**Lewis, C. S. *The Lion, the Witch and the Wardrobe.* New York: Collier/Macmillan, 1970. Study guide available from Mott Media (Milford, Mich.). Although children enjoy the video cartoon version, it is no substitute for the real thing. Many children will want to read, or hear read, the entire Chronicles of Narnia.

*MacDonald, George. *At the Back of the North Wind; The Princess and the Goblin; The Princess and Curdie.* London: Octopus, 1979. Complete and unabridged.

Mains, David and Karen. *Tales of the Kingdom.* Elgin, Ill.: Chariot/David C. Cook, 1983. The Chariot line is a good one.

Robinson, Barbara. *The Best Christmas Pageant Ever.* Illus. Judith Gwyn Brown. A top choice of everyone—non-Christians love the story, too. New York: Avon, 1987.

Speare, Elizabeth George. *The Bronze Bow.* Boston: Houghton Mifflin, 1961. Winner of the Newbery award. A story of conversion in the time of Christ. For older children.

Wangerin, Walter, Jr. *Potter: Come Fly to the First of the Earth.* Elgin, Ill.: Chariot/David C. Cook, 1985.

Biography:
Children should read Christian biographies. This is not a list, just

a few we have liked. Old ones are often the best—like Eaton's *Livingstone*. Read them before buying if you can; sometimes the Christianity is omitted or diluted, as in most biographies of Martin Luther King, Jr.

Eaton, Jeanette. *David Livingstone: Foe of Darkness*. New York: William Morrow, 1947.

De Paola, Tomie. *Francis: The Poor Man of Assisi*. New York: Holiday, 1982.

Peach, L. DuGarde. *Elizabeth Fry*. Loughborough, England: Ladybird, 1973.

Modern Theology, Philosophy, and Religion:

Some of these are controversial. Some are available in several editions. (See also *Classics*.)

Barth, Karl. *Church Dogmatics*. 4 vols. (in several bindings). Edinburgh: T & T Clark, 1936–1969.

Bonhoeffer, Dietrich. *The Cost of Discipleship*. New York: Macmillan, 1949.

__________. *Life Together*. New York: Harper & Row, 1954.

Bultmann, Rudolf. *Faith and Understanding*. Philadelphia: Fortress, 1987.

Chafer, Lewis Sperry. *Chafer's Systematic Theology*, abridged by John F. Walvoord, 2 vols. Wheaton, Ill.: Victor, 1988.

*Day, Millard F. *Basic Bible Doctrines*. Chicago: Moody, 1953.

Gamble, Harry Y. *The New Testament Canon: Its Making and Meaning*. Philadelphia: Fortress, 1985.

Kennedy, D. James. *Why I Believe.* Waco, Tex.: Word, 1980.

*Little, Paul E. *Know Why You Believe,* Rev. ed. Wheaton, Ill.: Victor, 1987.

Spurgeon, Charles. *All of Grace.* Pasadena, Tex.: Pilgrim Publications, 1978.

*Stott, John R. W. *Basic Christianity,* Downers Grove, Ill.: Inter-Varsity, 1958.

Teilhard de Chardin, Pierre. *The Divine Milieu.* New York: Harper & Row, 1965. Or read *The Phenomenon of Man.* New York: Harper & Row, 1959.

Other Nonfiction:

This is a potpourri, tendered as examples even though we may have omitted your personal favorites.

Brother Andrew. *God's Smuggler.* New York: New American, 1987.

Bellah, Robert, et al. *Habits of the Heart: Individualism & Commitment in American Life.* Berkeley: University of California, 1985.

Colson, Charles W. *Born Again.* Old Tappan, N.J.: Revell, 1976.

Fynn. *Mr. God, This Is Anna.* New York: Ballantine, 1974.

Elliot, Elisabeth. *Through Gates of Splendor.* Wheaton, Ill.: Tyndale, 1986.

Foster, Richard. *Celebration of Discipline.* New York: Harper, 1978. Study guide available.

Jones, E. Stanley. *Abundant Living.* Nashville: Abingdon, 1942.

Keller, Philip. *A Shepherd Looks at Psalm 23.* Grand Rapids, Mich.: Zondervan, 1976.

Kiemel, Ann. *I'm Out to Change My World.* Nashville, Tenn.: Impact, 1974.

King, Martin Luther, Jr. "I Have a Dream," in *Speeches by the Leaders: The March on Washington for Jobs and Freedom,* Aug. 28, 1963. New York: NAACP, 1963.

__________. *Strength to Love.* Philadelphia: Fortress, 1981.

LaHaye, Tim. *Spirit-Controlled Temperament.* Wheaton, Ill.: Tyndale, 1966.

Muggeridge, Malcolm. *Jesus: The Man Who Lives.* New York: Harper & Row, 1975.

Oursler, Fulton. *The Greatest Story Ever Told.* Garden City, N.Y.: Doubleday, 1949.

Peck, M. Scott. *The Road Less Traveled.* Old Tappan, N.J.: Simon & Schuster, 1980.

__________. *People of the Lie.* New York: Simon & Schuster, 1983.

Powell, John. *Why Am I Afraid to Love?* Niles, Ill: Argus, 1967.

Powers, J. F. *Presence of Grace.* Salem, N.H.: Ayer, 1956.

Richardson, Don. *Eternity in Their Hearts.* Ventura, Calif.: Regal/GL Publications, 1981.

Solzhenitsyn, Alexander. *Nobel Lecture [One Word of Truth].* Trans. F. D. Reeve. New York: Farrar, 1974.

Swindoll, Charles. *Strengthening Your Grip: Essentials in an Aimless World.* Waco, Tex.: Word, 1982.

ten Boom, Corrie, with John and Elizabeth Sherrill. *The Hiding Place.* Minneapolis: WorldWide, 1971.

Tournier, Paul. *The Whole Person in a Broken World: A Biblical Remedy for Today's World.* New York: Harper & Row, 1981.

__________. *The Meaning of Persons.* New York: Harper & Row, 1982.

Wilkerson, David. *The Cross and the Switchblade.* New York: Jove/Berkley, 1987.

Other Modern Fiction, Drama, and Poetry:

Faulkner, William. *The Sound and the Fury* and *As I Lay Dying.* New York: The Modern Library, 1946. Although Faulkner is not a Christian author, his portrait of the black Christian Dilsey in *The Sound and the Fury* is superb.

Hurnard, Hannah. *Hinds' Feet on High Places.* Wheaton, Ill.: Tyndale, 1979.

MacLeish, Archibald. *J. B.: A Play in Verse.* Boston: Houghton Mifflin, 1957. Modern retelling of Job story. Ending troubles some.

Miller, Arthur. *The Crucible.* New York: Viking, 1952. Strong, but ending is questionable for some.

Shaw, George Bernard. *St. Joan.* New York: Penguin, 1946. (*Androcles and the Lion* is also interesting, but comes out with all the wrong conclusions.)

Updike, John. *Rabbit, Run.* New York: Knopf, 1960. Some see interface with Christian values in this novel.

Reference and General:

The key to these is their accessibility. We keep ours in the living room.

**A complete Bible concordance
Many are finding computerized concordances easy to use. For books the old standards still are:

Cruden, A. M. *Cruden's Complete Concordance.*

Strong, James. *Strong's Exhaustive Concordance of the Bible.*

Young, Robert. *Young's Analytical Concordance of the Bible.*

*A church history—here are some examples:
Austin, Bill R. *Austin's Topical History of Christianity.* Wheaton, Ill.: Tyndale, 1983.

Dowley, Tim, ed. *Eerdmans' Handbook to the History of Christianity.* Grand Rapids, Mich.: Eerdmans, 1977.

Marty, Martin E. *A Short History of Christianity.* 2nd ed. Philadelphia: Fortress, 1987.

And maybe an Old Testament history:
Wood, Leon, and David O'Brien. *A Survey of Israel's History.* Rev. ed. Grand Rapids, Mich.: Zondervan, 1986.

A Bible handbook—two examples:
Halley, Henry H. *Halley's Bible Handbook.* Grand Rapids, Mich.: Zondervan, 1965.

Unger, Merrill. *New Unger's Bible Handbook.* Ed. Gary N. Larson. Rev. ed. Chicago: Moody, 1984.

*A Bible dictionary:
Douglas, J. D., ed. *The New Bible Dictionary.* Rev. ed. Wheaton, Ill.: Tyndale, 1982.

Gehman, Henry Snyder, ed. *The New Westminster Dictionary of the Bible*. Philadelphia: Westminster, 1970.

Vine, W. E. *Expository Dictionary of New Testament Words.*

A Bible atlas—two examples:

Beitzel, Barry. *The Moody Atlas of Bible Lands*. Chicago: Moody, 1985.

Pritchard, James B. *The Harper Atlas of the Bible*. New York: Harper & Row, 1987.

A Bible study book or study Bible:

a topical concordance (e.g., as in the Thompson Chain Reference Bibles)

Perhaps a short Bible commentary—here are some examples:

Carson, D. A. *New Testament Commentary Survey*. Grand Rapids, Mich.: Baker, 1986.

*Richards, Lawrence O. *The Teacher's Commentary*. Wheaton, Ill.: Victor, 1987.

Walvoord, John F., and Roy Zuck, eds. *The Bible Knowledge Commentary*, 2 vols. Wheaton, Ill.: Victor, 1983, 1985.

A survey, such as:

Gromacki, Robert G. *New Testament Survey*. Schaumburg, Ill.: Regular Bapt., 1974.

*A hymnbook (there are many to choose from).

Perhaps a book about worship, such as:

Allen, Ronald, and Gordon Borror. *Worship: Rediscovering the Missing Jewel*. Portland, Oreg.: Multnomah, 1982.

Martin, Ralph P. *Worship in the Early Church*. Westwood, N. J.: Revell, 1964.

Webber, Robert E. *Worship: Old and New*. Grand Rapids, Mich.: Zondervan, 1982. Or his *Worship Is a Verb*. Waco, Tex.: Word, 1985.

Some historical/archaeological picture books suitable for the coffee table, like these:

Masom, Caroline, and Pat Alexander, eds. *Picture Archive of the Bible*. Tring, England: Lion, 1987.

*Gower, Ralph. *The New Manners and Customs of Bible Times*. Chicago: Moody, 1987.

A book of Bible paintings (also suitable for the coffee table), like this one:

*Bruce, Bernard. *The Bible and Its Painters*. New York: Macmillan, 1983. One of the authors got an extra copy to cut up for prints.

Perhaps a literary guide to the Bible, such as:

Alter, Robert, and Frank Kermode, eds. *The Literary Guide to the Bible*. Cambridge, Mass.: Belknap, 1987.

Subscribe to a good all-around Christian magazine, like *Moody Monthly* or *Christianity Today*. You'd be surprised how much you can read during television commercials (or even programs) or before bed.

NOTES

Foreword

1. Bruno Bettelheim and Karen Zelan, *On Learning to Read: The Child's Fascination with Meaning* (New York: Knopf, 1982), 23.
2. E. D. Hirsch, Jr., *Cultural Literacy: What Every American Needs to Know* (Boston: Houghton Mifflin, 1987), xiii and xv.
3. Allan Bloom, *The Closing of the American Mind* (New York: Simon and Schuster, 1987), 380.

Chapter 1: Do Christians Know What They Need to Know?

1. Allan Bloom, *The Closing of the American Mind* (New York: Simon and Schuster, 1987); E. D. Hirsch, Jr., *Cultural Literacy: What Every American Needs to Know* (Boston: Houghton Mifflin, 1987).
2. Kenneth S. Kantzer, "What Happened in 586 B.C.?" *Christianity Today* (Mar. 4, 1988): 11.
3. Craig Dykstra, "Editorial: Memory and Truth," *Theology Today* (July 1987): 160.
4. Quoted by Richard Walker, "Trends: More Christians Saying No to Church," *Christianity Today* (Sept. 2, 1988): 57.
5. Hirsch, *Cultural Literacy*, 2.
6. Ibid., xiii and xv.
7. For summaries of the many studies documenting the erosion of basic knowledge among young people, see David Gates, "A Dunce Cap for America," *Newsweek* (Apr. 20, 1987): 72–74; and Alvin P. Sanoff, "What Americans Should Know," *U.S. News & World Report* (Sept. 28, 1987): 86–94.
8. Kantzer, "What Happened in 586 B.C.?" 11.

Chapter 2: Is Christian Knowledge Important?

1. Whorf's original hypothesis can be found in Benjamin Lee Whorf, *Language, Thought, and Reality* (Cambridge, Mass.: MIT

Press, 1956).

2. A typical Lewis explanation contrasts the model held by the Middle Ages with our own: "We can no longer dismiss the change of Models as a simple progress from error to truth. . . . Each is a serious attempt to get in all the phenomena known at a given period, and each succeeds in getting in a great many. But also, no less surely, each reflects the prevalent psychology of an age almost as much as it reflects the state of that age's knowledge. . . . It is not impossible that our own Model will die a violent death, ruthlessly smashed by an unprovoked assault of new facts." From C. S. Lewis, *The Discarded Image: An Introduction to Medieval and Renaissance Literature* (Cambridge, England: Cambridge University Press, 1964), 222.

3. Study conducted by Bruce Hicks, academic dean, Friends Bible College, Haviland, Kansas.

4. Issac Newton, quoted in *Familar Quotations* by John Bartlett (Boston: Little, Brown and Company, 1968), 379; and Saint Bernard of Clairvaux, *Works*, quoted in an advertisement for *Christian History* magazine, *Christianity Today* (Feb. 3, 1989): back cover.

5. "Taizé: That Little Springtime," Martin Doblmeier, producer and director (Mt. Vernon, Va.: Journey Communications, Ltd.).

6. William Lambdin, ed., s.v. "born again," *Doublespeak Dictionary* (Los Angeles: Pinnacle, 1979).

7. "The fact is that memorizing has [a] . . . very profound value. As poet Richard Wilbur put the matter in a poetry course in which he required memorization, one takes the poem to heart, makes it a part of oneself." See James Moffett and Betty Jane Wagner, *Student-Centered Language Arts and Reading, K–13: A Handbook for Teachers*, 3d ed. (Boston: Houghton Mifflin, 1983), 263. The earliest edition, without a coauthor, broke ground for the new learning concepts Moffett championed.

8. Robert E. Coleman, *The Master Plan of Evangelism* (Old Tappan, N.J.: Revell, 1964), 39–40.

Chapter 3: How Can We Find What Is Essential?

1. An example of the "red line" is "The Scarlet Thread of Redemption" from the Open Bible of the KJV (Nashville: Thomas

Nelson, 1975), 1249.

2. Quoted by Betsy Rubiner, "Writing's Writing," *Wichita Eagle-Beacon* (Sept. 25, 1988): E2. L'Engle won the Newbery medal for the best children's book for 1963, *A Wrinkle in Time* (New York: Scholastic, 1962).

3. Leland Ryken, *Windows to the World: Literature in Christian Perspective* (Grand Rapids, Mich.: Zondervan Publishing House, 1985), 62.

4. C. S. Lewis, *Mere Christianity* (New York: Macmillan, 1952), 6.

5. *Christianity Today* (Oct. 21, 1988): 43.

6. Quoted by Emmet John Hughes, "The Sword of Christianity," *The World's Great Religions* (New York: Time-Life Books, 1957), 248.

7. Alan Johnson, professor of biblical studies and ethics at Wheaton College, participating in a dialogue of evangelicals and Jews that was reported in " 'Fulfilled Jews' or 'Former Jews'?" *Christianity Today* (Oct. 7, 1988): 68.

8. Clyde Kilby, unpublished lecture notes, Wheaton (Ill.) College.

Chapter 4: What Do You Know? Test Yourself

Answers to Tests

Test 1: Common Bible Sayings I

1. keeper; 2. lions'; 3. others; 4. die; 5. brother; 6. world; 7. way; 8. house; 9. honey; 10. treasures; 11. faith; 12. room; 13. love (or charity); 14. children; 15. other; 16. faith; 17. Train; 18. sheep; 19. doers; 20. heart

Test 2: About the Bible

1. Jesus said it to Nicodemus (John 3:3).

2. Matthew, Mark, Luke, John.

3. 66.

4. God the Father, the Son (i.e., Jesus), and the Holy Spirit (Holy Ghost).

5. John 11:35, "Jesus wept."

6. "Do unto others as you would have others do unto you" (Proverbial version of Luke 6:31). (Give yourself credit if you had the gist of it.)

7. Psalms (150).
8. The correct answer is "Neither." Hezekiah was a king, not a book of the Bible.
9. The Pentateuch.
10. "Go ye therefore, and teach all nations, baptizing them in the name of the Father, and of the Son, and of the Holy Ghost: teaching them to observe all things whatsoever I have commanded you" (Matt. 28:19–20).

Test 3: In the Bible

1–4. Matthew, Mark, Luke, John; 5. Luke; 6. Satan/Devil; 7. Lot's wife; 8–12. Genesis, Exodus, Leviticus, Numbers, Deuteronomy; 13. Benjamin; 14. manna; 15. Saul; 16. Bethlehem; 17. Jezebel; 18. "Love your neighbor as yourself" (Mark 12:31); 19. Jacob; 20. the Red Sea

Test 4: People

1. J; 2. H; 3. L; 4. G; 5. N; 6. I; 7. A; 8. K; 9. F; 10. M; 11. E; 12. O; 13. D; 14. B; 15. C

Test 5: Terms and Phrases

1. C; 2. A; 3. B; 4. A (Traditionally, Ecclesiastes is attributed to Solomon. All the book itself claims for an author is "the Preacher."); 5. C; 6. A; 7. C; 8. C; 9. D; 10. C; 11. D; 12. A; 13. B; 14. D; 15. B; 16. C; 17. A; 18. D; 19. C; 20. C

Test 6: Common Bible Sayings II

1. sting; 2. light; 3. myrrh; 4. life; 5. world; 6. God; 7. keep; 8. beginning; 9. faith; 10. temptation; 11. bread; 12. love; 13. Father; 14. strength; 15. sins; 16. shadow; 17. death; 18. reap; 19. truth, truth; 20. Omega

Test 7: Geography

1. M; 2. E; 3. L; 4. J; 5. H; 6. D; 7. A; 8. N; 9. O; 10. F; 11. B; 12. C; 13. G; 14. K; 15. I

Test 8: Sayings that May Surprise You

1. not done (or left undone); 2. riches (wrong answer given: ointment); 3. grace (wrong answer given: work); 4. disposes; 5. wife

(wrong answer given: woman); 6. horsemen (wrong answers given: horses, angels); 7. ant (wrong answer given: devil); 8. prophet; 9. Abandon hope, all ye who enter here (wrong answer given: Abandon all hope, ye who enter here); 10. beautiful; 11. battle; 12. trust in (wrong answer given: praise); 13. more blessed (wrong answer given: better); 14. good; 15. glory; 16. Love (wrong answer given: pray for); 17. Pride goes before *destruction,* and a haughty spirit before a fall. (Wrong answer given: a fall); 18. The love of money (wrong answer given: Money); 19. seen; 20. death; 21. leopard, kid (wrong answer given: lion, lamb); 22. hateth his son. (Wrong answer given: spoils the child); 23. Wounded; 24. Lucifer; 25. dwelling place *or* tabernacles (KJV) (Wrong answers given: promises, precepts, feet, mercies).

Test 9: Ten Commandments (Exod. 20:2–17, KJV)
Give yourself credit if you have the gist of these.

1. Thou shalt have no other gods besides me.
2. Thou shalt not worship any graven image.
3. Thou shalt not take the name of the Lord thy God in vain.
4. Remember the sabbath day to keep it holy.
5. Honor thy father and mother.
6. Thou shalt not kill.
7. Thou shalt not commit adultery.
8. Thou shalt not steal.
9. Thou shalt not bear false witness.
10. Thou shalt not covet.

Test 10: Beatitudes (Matt. 5:3–12, KJV)
Give yourself credit if you have the gist of these.

1. Blessed are the poor in spirit . . .
2. Blessed are they that mourn. . . .
3. Blessed are the meek. . . .
4. Blessed are they which do hunger and thirst after righteousness. . . .
5. Blessed are the merciful. . . .
6. Blessed are the pure in heart. . . .

7. Blessed are the peacemakers. . . .
8. Blessed are they which are persecuted for righteousness' sake. . . .
9. Blessed are ye, when men shall revile you, and persecute you. . . .

Test 11: Fruit of the Spirit (Gal. 5:22–24, KJV plus synonyms)
1. love (regard, admiration, affection, tenderness)
2. joy (happiness, delight, mirth)
3. peace (friendship, harmony, repose, concord)
4. longsuffering (forbearance, patience)
5. gentleness (kindness, mildness)
6. goodness (virtue, excellence, worth, welfare, generosity)
7. faith (trust, reliance, confidence, faithfulness, fidelity)
8. meekness (humbleness, submissiveness, gentleness)
9. temperance (moderation, self-denial, restraint, self-control)

Test 12: Christ's Seven Last Words from the Cross (Matt. 27, Luke 23, John 19, KJV)
Give yourself credit if you have the gist of these.

1. "Father, forgive them; they know not what they do."
2. "Today thou shalt be with me in Paradise."
3. "Woman, behold thy son." To John, "Behold thy mother."
4. "My God, my God, why hast thou forsaken me?"
5. "I thirst."
6. "It is finished."
7. "Father, into thy hands I commend my spirit."

Test 13: Seven Deadly Sins (with synonyms)
1. pride (vanity, arrogance, conceit); 2. lust (passion, craving); 3. envy (jealousy, resentment); 4. anger (wrath, rage, fury); 5. covetousness (avarice, greed); 6. gluttony (insatiability, piggishness); 7. sloth (laziness, idleness)

Test 14: Armor of God (Eph. 6:13–17, KJV)
Give yourself credit if you have the gist of these.

1. belt of truth; 2. breastplate of righteousness; 3. feet shod with the preparation of the gospel of peace; 4. shield of faith; 5. helmet of salvation; 6. sword of the Spirit, which is the Word of God

Test 15: Post-biblical Christians
1. B; 2. C; 3. D; 4. B; 5. D; 6. A; 7. D; 8. A; 9. B; 10. A; 11. B; 12. D; 13. B; 14. C; 15. A

Test 16: Biblical Allusions in a Contemporary Speech (Martin Luther King, Jr.: "I Have a Dream")
Drawn from Martin Luther King, Jr., "I Have a Dream" in *Speeches by the Leaders: The March on Washington for Jobs and Freedom,* August 28, 1963 (New York: NAACP, 1963).

Are these italicized and bracketed phrases the allusions and quotations you found?

Five score years ago, a great American, in whose symbolic shadow we stand today, signed the Emancipation Proclamation. . . . It came as the joyous daybreak [echo of 2 Pet. 1:19, etc.] to end the long night of *captivity* [cf. Egyptian and Babylonian captivities]. . . .

Now is the time to rise from the *dark* and desolate *valley* [echo of Ps. 23] of segregation to the sunlit path of racial justice. Now is the time to lift our nation from the quicksands of racial injustice to the solid *rock* [Ps. 40] of *brotherhood* [1 Pet. 2:17, etc.]. Now is the time to make justice a reality for all of *God's children* [Matt. 5:9, etc.].

. . . The whirlwinds [echo of Zech. 9:14, etc.] of revolt will continue to shake the foundations of our nation until the bright day of justice emerges [hint of Isa. 62:1, etc.].

. . . Let us not seek to *satisfy our thirst* [echo of Jer. 2:13, 25, etc.] for freedom by *drinking from the cup* [echo of Rev. 8:11, 16:19, etc.] of bitterness and hatred.

. . . No, no, we are not satisfied and we will not be satisfied until *justice rolls down like the waters and righteousness like a mighty stream* [Amos 5:24].

I am not unmindful that some of you have come here *out of great* trials and *tribulations* [Rev. 7:14]. . . . Continue to work with the faith that *unearned suffering* [1 Pet. 3:14, 17] is redemptive.

. . . I say to you today, my friends, even though we face the difficulties of today and tomorrow, I still have a dream. . . . I have a dream that one day this nation will rise up and live out the true meaning of its creed: "We hold these truths to be self-evident that all *men are created* [Gen. 1:27] equal."

. . . I have a dream that one day down in Alabama . . . little black boys and black girls will be able to join hands with little white boys and white girls as *sisters and brothers* [James 2:15, etc.].

. . . I have a dream that one day *every valley shall be exalted, every hill and mountain shall be made low, the rough places will be made plain and the crooked places will be made straight, and the glory of the Lord shall be revealed, and all flesh shall see it together* [Isa. 40].

This is our hope. . . . With this faith we will be able to work together, to pray together, to struggle together, to go to jail together, to stand up for freedom together, knowing that we will be free one day [hint of John 8:32, etc.].

This will be the day when all of *God's children* [Matt. 5:9, etc.] will be able to sing with new meaning: "My country 'tis of thee, / Sweet land of liberty, [hint of Lev. 25:10, etc.] / Of thee I sing: . . ."

From every mountainside, let freedom ring. And when we allow freedom to ring, when we let it ring from every village, from every hamlet, from every state and every city, we will be able to speed up that day when all of God's children, black men and white men, Jews and Gentiles, Protestants and Catholics, will be able to join hands [echo of Gal. 3:28] and sing in the words of the old Negro spirtual: "Free at last! free at last! thank God almighty, we are free at last!"

Chapter 5: What Do Literate Christians Know?

1. Dick Cavalli, "Winthrop," *NEA* (Nov. 6, 1988). Most people we showed this cartoon to didn't know why it was funny. *Apocryphal* is on our list as well as on Hirsch's list in *Cultural Literacy: What Every American Needs to Know* (Boston: Houghton Mifflin, 1987).

2. C. H. Spurgeon, *Autobiography, Volume I: The Early Years, 1834–1859*, quoted in Gary Inrig, *Quality Friendship* (Chicago: Moody, 1981), 178. Spurgeon said he "there and then . . . determined . . . to . . . preach . . . the Word so long as I had strength to do it."

3. John Woolman, *The Journal of John Woolman* in George McMichael, ed., *Anthology of American Literature*, 3rd ed., vol. 1: Colonial through Romantic (New York: Macmillan, 1985), 223–24.

4. Robert H. Schuller, *Your Church Has a Fantastic Future: A*

Possibility Thinker's Guide to a Successful Church (Ventura, Calif: Regal, 1986), 261.

5. Rachel's household gods are called *teraphim* (Gen. 31:19, 34); teraphim are also mentioned in Judges 17:5; 18:14, 20; Hosea 3:4. *Seraphim* are from Isaiah 6:2, 6. The line in the hymn "Holy, Holy, Holy" by Reginald Heber and John B. Dykes is "Cherubim and seraphim falling down before Thee. . . ."; it is found in most hymnals.

6. Hirsch, *Cultural Literacy,* 146.

7. Median age: forty-eight. Education: 82 percent are college graduates; 71 percent attended graduate school; 52 percent have a graduate degree. Theological or doctrinal preference: evangelical, 54 percent; conservative, 14 percent; fundamental, 9 percent; charismatic, 6 percent; traditional, confessional, 6 percent; other, 11 percent.

8. Colson writes in his best-selling autobiography how Christ overwhelmed him as he read *Mere Christianity:* Charles W. Colson, *Born Again* (Old Tappan, N. J.: Revell, 1977), 112ff. Hatfield's conversion, he himself says, was a gradual transformation that came when he realized, "I'd have to make a choice. I began to pray and read an hour every night—the Bible and books like those of C. S. Lewis" "Decisions for Christ," *Newsweek* (Oct. 25, 1976): 75.

9. Jonathan Zimmerman, Special, *Baltimore Evening Sun,* distributed by the Los Angeles Times—Washington Post News Service, "Could Kitty and Barbara Be Mary and Martha?" *Seattle Times/Seattle Post-Intelligencer* (July 24, 1988): A18. Mary and Martha are characterized in Luke 10:38–42 and John 11–12:11.

10. Ibid. "Weaker vessel" is not a mere popular proverb for weak women; Peter's application is much wider, for he says all wives are to be given honor "as unto the weaker vessel," although many Christians we tested do not recognize that anymore, possibly because the NIV drops the term, using "weaker partner" (1 Pet. 3:7).

11. Lou Christen, letter to the editor, "Mary and Martha: What's Next? How Abel Bumped Off Cain?" *Seattle Times/Seattle Post-Intelligencer* (July 31, 1988): A19.

12. Malcolm Muggeridge, "A Skeptic Goes to Bethlehem," condensed from *Jesus: The Man Who Lives* (New York: Harper, 1975) in *Reader's Digest* (Dec. 1988): 163.

Chapter 6: Has the Torch Been Passed or Dropped?

1. Virginia Stem Owens, "God and Man at Texas A&M," *The Reformed Journal* (Nov. 1987): 3–4.
2. David Gates, "A Dunce Cap for America," *Newsweek* (Apr. 20, 1987): 72.
3. Ibid.
4. This is true even though she—71 percent were women—was somewhat self-selecting and probably more confident that she knew the answers than the four out of five who did not respond to the *Campus Life* survey, and even though half the respondents were attending college or were graduated from college. The most frequent theological or doctrinal preference was *evangelical*, 33 percent. Out of five hundred surveys mailed, one hundred *Campus Life* subscribers responded. It must be emphasized that the results from the younger respondents were skewed *in favor* of a positive response: Only one out of five responded, which can be interpreted as both higher interest and higher knowledge than the four out of five who did not, and the subscribers to this magazine are likely to be active Christians.
5. A 1980 survey by 1,003 telephone interviews was conducted by Gallup for the Washington, D.C.–based Center for Applied Research in the Apostolate (CARA) and reported in Princeton Religion Research Center's *Emerging Trends* (Apr. 1988): 2. See also Richard Walker, "More Christians Saying No to Church," *Christianity Today* (Sept. 2, 1988): 57.
6. Susan Littwin, *The Postponed Generation* (New York: Morrow, 1987), as quoted by William H. Willimon, "Risky Business," *Christianity Today* (Feb. 19, 1988): 24.
7. Mark Wade, Chairman of Christian Education, Friends Bible College, Haviland, Kansas; interviewed by Jo H. Lewis, fall 1988. The other side is pointed out by missionary candidate Jeff Hause of Clearwater, Florida: "But with such a fast-paced change in culture and society, how can we abandon age grouping and effectively teach? Can we devise ways to segment and [still] gain community?"
8. Howard Macy, "Fixing Education," *Evangelical Friend* (Feb. 1984): 28.
9. James Michael Lee, *The Shape of Religious Instruction* (Misha-

waka, Ind.: Religious Education Press, 1971).

10. This is the lesson of C. S. Lewis's tool shed. C. S. Lewis, *The Business of Heaven: Daily Readings from C. S. Lewis*, ed. Walter Hooper (San Diego: Harcourt Brace Jovanovich, 1984), 196–200.

11. Allan Bloom, *The Closing of the American Mind* (New York: Simon and Schuster, 1987).

12. Ibid., 68, 73–74.

13. Tim Stafford in Philip Yancey and Tim Stafford, "The Research Was Right . . ." Advertisement, *Christianity Today* (July 15, 1988): 64.

14. This finding comes from a major study, *The Unchurched American, 1988*, quoted in Princeton Religion Research Center's *Emerging Trends* (Oct. 1988): 1.

15. James Dobson, *Dr. Dobson Answers Your Questions* (Wheaton, Ill.: Tyndale House, 1983), quoted in *Dr. James Dobson's Focus on the Family Bulletin* (Oct. 1988).

16. Paul C. Vitz, *Censorship: Evidence of Bias in Our Children's Textbooks* (Ann Arbor, Mich.: Servant, 1986), 1–2.

17. Bryce Christensen, "School Prayers in the Literature Class," Ibid., 122. Cf. Paul Vitz, *Psychology as Religion: The Cult of Self-Worship* (Grand Rapids, Mich: Eerdmans, 1977).

18. Kenneth L. Woodward, "Born Again!" *Newsweek* (Oct. 25, 1976): 68–78; the article cites on page 68 the Gallup poll figures about the born-again Americans, "based on personal interviews with 1,553 Americans of voting age." The 1988 statistics are from Walker, "More Christians," 57.

19. Tim Stafford, "Roberta Hestenes: Taking Charge," *Christianity Today* (Mar. 3, 1989): 16–22. She is the president of Eastern College, St. Davids, Pennsylvania.

20. Jerry Bridges, *The Pursuit of Holiness* (Colorado Springs, Colo.: NavPress, 1978).

21. This is the Chancel Choir, First Presbyterian Church, Arlington Heights, Illinois.

Chapter 7: What Must We Do?

1. Review of Diane Ravitch and Chester E. Finn, Jr., *What Do Our*

17-Year-Olds Know? A Report on the First National Assessment of History and Literature (New York: Harper, 1987) in *New Oxford Review* (Sept. 1988): 32. An example of knowledge that did not lead to morality and civil sanity is Joseph Stalin, who as a young man studied for the priesthood. See *World Encyclopedia*, 1967 ed., s.v. "Stalin, Joseph," by Myron Rush.

2. Quoted by Elizabeth Greene, "Proponent of 'Cultural Literacy' Finds Disciples in the Nation's Schools," *The Chronicle of Higher Education* (Nov. 16, 1988): A17.

3. Douglas Groothuis, "Confronting the New Age," *Christianity Today* (Jan. 13, 1989): 39.

4. David Awbrey, "Loss of Leisure: 'Acceleration Syndrome' Sends Holidays Scurrying By," *Wichita Eagle-Beacon* (Nov. 27, 1988): 3B.

5. In youth groups often two-thirds would say they had started, but only one or two individuals would have finished, say Philip Yancey and Tim Stafford, "The Research Was Right! . . ." Advertisement for the NIV Student Bible, *Christianity Today* (July 15, 1988): 64.

6. Tim Stafford, "Opening the Closed Book," *Christianity Today* (Apr. 4, 1986): 26.

7. As quoted by David Neff, "Sunday School and the B-I-B-L-E," *Christianity Today* (Apr. 4, 1986): 27.

8. "The Story of Raising a Pastoral Family: An Interview with David and Helen Seamands," *Leadership* (Fall 1981): 19.

9. One helpful reference is "Scriptural Allusions in Hymns," *Hymns for the Family of God* (Nashville: Paragon Associates, 1976), 707. Many hymnbooks have such indexes in the back.

10. "Religious Training at Home a Key Factor in Future Church Involvement," Princeton Religious Research Council's *Emerging Trends* (Oct. 1988). The finding comes from a survey entitled *The Unchurched American, 1988*.

11. Phil George, "Season of Grandmothers." Quoted at the Nez Percé National Historical Park, Spalding, Idaho.

12. William Gibson, *The Miracle Worker* (New York: Bantam, 1984). Emphasis ours.

13. Bruno Bettelheim, *The Uses of Enchantment; The Meaning and Importance of Fairy Tales* (New York: Knopf, 1976).

14. John Woolman, from *The Journal of John Woolman* in George McMichael, ed., *Anthology of American Literature,* 3rd ed., vol. 1: Colonial through Romantic (New York: Macmillan, 1985), 223–25.

15. Laurence Sombke, "How Our Meals Have Changed," *USA Weekend* (Nov. 11–13, 1988): 4.

16. This is from the final poem of "God's Determinations," a cycle of poems that moves from God's power in the "Preface" to the elect's heavenly journey, written about 1685. Taylor was an American frontier Puritan pastor who lived from 1645 to 1729 and whose poetry was not published until 1939. The horse-drawn coach is Christ's church; today that could be a car, or, as Meeter says, a jetliner or a rocket. Merle Meeter, anthologist, *Major American Authors to Twain: With Biblical, Theocentric Critique,* vol. 1: Bradford through Whittier, unpublished, 1979, 30. The poem is on p. 34.

17. See note 10 above.

18. *This Is the Way We Teach Babies, Toddlers, and Twos.* Film from Dalma Smiley, Box 64608, Lubbock, Texas 79464.

19. Stafford, "Opening," 28.

20. *Through the Bible: Daily Readings Covering the Entire Bible* for each year is available from the National Association of Evangelicals, P.O. Box 28, Wheaton, Illinois, 60189. *The One Year Bible: Arranged in 365 Daily Readings: The New International Version* (Wheaton, Ill.: Tyndale House Publishers, 1986).

21. P. I. D., "Get You a Bible" on the audio cassette *Here We Are* (Houston: Star Song Records, 1988).

22. "Praise for All Seasons," an original concept, was presented in March 1987 by a church that went through the seasons (Advent, Christmas, Epiphany, Easter, Pentecost, and the Second Coming) in music and narration in a single service. Allen Pote, *A Season to Celebrate* (Chapel Hill, N.C.: Hinshaw Music, 1984).

23. Even independent evangelical churches are recovering the tradition of Lent through such resources as *50 Day Spiritual Adventures,* sponsored by the Chapel of the Air, Box 30, Wheaton, Ill. 60189-0030.

24. Walter Wangerin, Jr., "Telling Tales," *Publishers Weekly* (Mar. 7, 1986): 40; and Wangerin, "Practicing the Oral Tradition," Friends University's Ministers' Seminar Series, October 13, 1988, Wichita, Kansas.

25. D. Bruce Lockerbie, "A Cure for Biblical Illiteracy," a review of Robert Alter and Frank Kermode, eds., *The Literary Guide to the Bible* (Cambridge, Mass.: Belknap, 1987) in *Christianity Today* (Sept. 16, 1988): 51.

Chapter 8: What Will Happen?

1. Review of Diane Ravitch and Chester D. Finn, Jr., *What Do Our 17-Year-Olds Know? A Report on the First National Assessment of History and Literature* (New York: Harper and Row, 1987) in *New Oxford Review* (Sept. 1988): 32. We cannot pass up this opportunity to identify the literary allusion. Cassandra was the Greek princess in Homer who prophesied doom truly but was never believed, not too unlike Jeremiah and Ezekiel.

2. C. S. Lewis, *The Lion, the Witch and the Wardrobe* (New York: Collier, 1950).

3. Nancy Shulins, "Homeless Hero Finds New Hope," *Wichita Eagle-Beacon* (Feb. 26, 1989): 1E, 4E.

4. Lisa Anderson, "The Death of the Yuppie," *Wichita Eagle-Beacon* (Dec. 13, 1987): 1D, 6D. Elkins is "president of the Naisbitt Group, a Washington, D.C.–based research and consulting business specializing in social forecasting."

5. Ann Japenga, Los Angeles Times—Washington Post News Service, "Yuppies Go Home—to Church," *Wichita Eagle-Beacon* (June 4, 1988): 6E, 7E. Japenga also notes that older baby boomers, born 1945 to 1955, are starting to attend worship regularly, according to a study by the Center for Social and Religious Research, Hartford (Conn.) Seminary—from 1974 to 1984, the increase was 10 percent.

6. Ibid.

7. Robert N. Bellah, et al., *Habits of the Heart: Individualism and Commitment in American Life* (New York: Harper & Row, 1986); M. Scott Peck, *People of the Lie: The Hope for Healing Human Evil* (Simon and Schuster, 1983).

8. Dan Wakefield, "We Need More Religion in Prime Time," *TV Guide* (Mar. 11, 1989): 15–16.

9. Richard Walker, "Trends: More Christians Saying No to

Church," *Christianity Today* (Sept. 2, 1988): 57.

10. Tom Schafer, " 'Black & White Together': When Will We Practice What We Preach?" *Wichita Eagle-Beacon* (Jan. 15, 1989): 1C.

11. David Neff, "Sunday School and the B-I-B-L-E," *Christianity Today* (Apr. 4, 1986): 27.

12. Japenga, "Yuppies," 7E. Medved is a writer and movie critic as well as president of the Pacific Jewish Center in Venice, a Los Angeles community.

13. Virginia Stem Owens, "God and Man at Texas A&M," *The Reformed Journal* (Nov. 1987): 4.

14. Beverly LaHaye, "Education in the Year 2020: What Will Our Children Learn?" *Concerned Women* (Sept. 1988): 6.

15. Ibid.

16. D. Bruce Lockerbie, "A Cure for Biblical Illiteracy," a review of Robert Alter and Frank Kermode, eds., *The Literary Guide to the Bible* (Cambridge, Mass.: Belknap, 1987) in *Christianity Today* (Sept. 16, 1988): 51.

17. Quoted in Joe Maxwell, "Will Sunday School Survive?" *Christianity Today* (Dec. 9, 1988): 64.

18. Ray Bradbury, *Fahrenheit 451* (Westminster, Md.: Ballantine, 1967).

19. Psychologist Vicki Ramsey, Houston, Texas.

20. See Carl F. H. Henry, *Twilight of a Great Civilization: The Drift Toward Neo-Paganism* (Westchester, Ill.: Crossway Books, 1988).

21. Tim Stafford, "Opening the Closed Book," *Christianity Today* (Apr. 4, 1986): 28.

Appendix 1: What Christians Should Know: A Preliminary List

1. E. D. Hirsch, Jr., *Cultural Literacy: What Every American Needs to Know* (Boston: Houghton Mifflin, 1987), 152–215.

2. Hirsch also had "a southerly one, below which lies knowledge so obvious and widely known that its inclusion would make the list unusably long." But we tended to ignore the southerly border almost completely, for that would cut out "the heart of the core" of Christianity. See Hirsch, *Cultural Literacy*, 138.

3. Ibid.
4. Ibid., 142.
5. Ibid., 127.
6. Ibid., 150.

Appendix 2: Suggested Reading List

1. Allan Bloom, "A Book Can Transform a Life," *U.S. News & World Report* (Sept. 28, 1987): 95.